MARVEL

CAPTAIN MARVEL

In a story that takes place on Earth in the 1990s and in the midst of an epic space war, the mysterious origins of Captain Marvel are revealed.

The cast and crew of the movie look at the creation of a groundbreaking new chapter in the Marvel Cinematic Universe...

TITAN EDITORIAL
Editor **Jonathan Wilkins**
Managing Editor **Martin Eden**
Assistant Editors **Tolly Maggs &**
Jake Devine
Senior Designer **Andrew Leung**
Art Director **Oz Browne**
Senior Production Controller **Jackie Flook**
Production Controller **Peter James**
Sales & Circulation Manager **Steve Tothill**
Senior Brand Manager **Chris Thompson**

Senior Publicist **Will O'Mullane**
Publicist **Imogen Harris**
Advertising Assistant **Bella Hoy**
Commercial Manager **Michelle Fairlamb**
Publishing Manager **Darryl Tothill**
Publishing Director **Chris Teather**
Operations Director **Leigh Baulch**
Executive Director **Vivian Cheung**
Publisher **Nick Landau**

DISTRIBUTION
US Newsstand: **Total Publisher Services, Inc.**
John Dziewiatkowski, 630-851-7683
US Newsstand Distribution **Curtis Circulation Company**
US Bookstore Distribution **The News Group**
US Direct Sales: **Diamond Comic Distributors**

For more info on advertising contact
adinfo@titanemail.com
Marvel Studios' *Captain Marvel* published March 2019 by Titan Magazines, a division of Titan Publishing Group Limited, 144 Southwark Street, London SE1 0UP.

For sale in the U.S. and Canada.

Printed in the US by Quad
ISBN: 9781785868054

Contributor **Nick Jones**

Thank you to Christopher Troise, Shiho Tilley, and Eugene Paraszczuk at Disney for all their help.

Titan Authorized User. No part of this publication may be reproduced, stored in a retrival system, or transmitted, in any form or by any means, without the prior written permission of the publisher. A CIP catalogue record for this title is available from the British Library.

10 9 8 7 6 5 4 3 2 1

MARVEL
© 2019 MARVEL

Contents

Anna Boden and Ryan Fleck

The Directors

Directing team Anna Boden and Ryan Fleck make the leap from indie classics *It's Kind of a Funny Story* and *Mississippi Grind* to big budget adventure of the Marvel Cinematic Universe.

Captain Marvel: The Official Movie Special: When did you first become aware of the Marvel Cinematic Universe?

Anna Boden: My first experience was *Iron Man* in 2008. Ryan and I had been Robert Downey Jr. fans for a long time. He was the first person we wanted to cast on our very first feature film. It totally amazed us that he was cast as a Super Hero – it was such a bold move. *Iron Man* was the first Super Hero movie that I really loved as an adult.

Ryan Fleck: The humor in it felt very grounded and he was a grounded character. It's based in a world that feels familiar and is earthbound. It's Tony Stark's suit that has the powers.

AB: The writers weren't afraid to push his likability. When you have somebody like Downey Jr. who is so charming and has so much depth as an actor, you can do that and still keep an audience. He can be darker at the beginning so it's a big swing when he becomes a hero. Before we started

> ## "We are getting to create this Super Hero who is a very powerful human being who's complicated and has flaws."
> ### - Anna Boden

doing this movie and we were trying to get actors for our indie films, we would look at who was available and our favorite actors would all be busy doing Marvel movies!

Is Marvel Studios supportive of the "human element first and spectacle second" approach?

RF: 100 percent. The fact that Marvel called us to even have a conversation about doing a movie like this shows how seriously it's taking character-oriented filmmakers like Taika Waititi and Ryan Coogler.

What attracted you to *Captain Marvel*?

AB: What attracted us to the project was the character of Carol Danvers. We particularly loved (comic book writer) Kelly Sue DeConnick's run. We really fell in love with that take on the character, her humor, her humanity, her need to prove herself and all of that swagger that comes from an Air Force background.

How did you approach the story for this film?

AB: We're tackling this origin story from a slightly different angle, not only because it sets up the entire Marvel Cinematic Universe – this is a pre-*Iron Man* universe that we're exploring – but also because we're not meeting her as a human and following a linear trajectory to her becoming a Super Hero. We have mixed it up a little bit and jumped ahead in time. This story tells how she gets from being a human fighter pilot to becoming this powerful alien warrior who shoots photon blasts from her hands. We skip that part in the beginning, and then we uncover it over the course of the movie. It's a story of self-discovery for her. Being a fighter pilot is such an important part of who she is.

When she is an alien warrior who comes to Earth, she meets Nick Fury. It's the interaction with her over the course of the movie that makes him realize that there's a whole universe out there where there are aliens who cause crazy intergalactic wars.

RF: We have to take the whole MCU into consideration

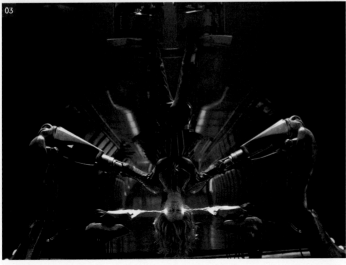

with any of these characters, but especially Nick Fury who was there from the beginning, putting the Avengers together. Meeting her is what inspires him to put together a group to protect Earth from these other forces.

AB: What's really fun about seeing Nick Fury more than a decade before *Iron Man* is that we get to see a little bit of who this guy was before he was the super cool agent who we meet in the later movies. We see him getting his eyes opened for the first time and experiencing things that he had no idea about. Fury and Captain Marvel share a journey over the course of the film.

RF: Yeah, and he's got two eyes!

Talk about the impact for you of introducing this female Super Hero character?

AB: It's amazing to get the opportunity to introduce this character to so many people, not only because she is one of the most powerful characters in the Marvel Universe and because she's a woman, but also because she's a character that a hardcore group of fans know really well.

We are getting to create this Super Hero who is a very powerful human being who's complicated and has flaws, doubts, and insecurities just like all of us do. We have a picture of the cover of one of the comics in our office that shows a little girl in a Captain Marvel uniform flying ▶

01 Ryan Fleck and Anna Boden direct actor Ben Mendelsohn

02 Brie Larson goes before the camera

03 Danvers finds herself in a very alien world

04 Boden and Larson in conference as they work out a scene

05 Carol Danvers: one of the most powerful heroes in the Marvel Cinematic Universe.

> "We had to de-age Samuel L. Jackson a little bit. He didn't need much — we ran some tests and the guy looks good!"
> - Ryan Fleck

▶ through the sky, and it reminds us who we're making the movie for and who we want to inspire with this movie.

What does Brie Larson bring to the role?
AB: I'm such a fan of her acting. She's so strong and she brings such a range of emotion to all the characters that she plays. She actually is a really powerful human being aside from what she does on the screen. She's not afraid to speak her mind and she's really funny. She looks really good in that costume.
RF: She was here before us. She's part of the reason we're here. We're big fans. She has a huge body of work, but we saw her in a movie called *Short Term 12*, which was fantastic, and she really just took it to another level with *Room*. We couldn't wait to work with her.

What kind of character is Carol Danvers?
AB: She has a lot of swagger, and a real sense of humor. She's a fighter pilot in the Air Force, so she has that kind of *Top Gun*/Maverick attitude. Part of that comes from a deep-seated need to prove herself, which comes from having some self–doubt and fear. Does she become humble? Does she end the movie with any less swagger than she began

it with? She's always going to have that as part of who she is.

Was the 1990s setting your idea?
RF: It's necessary for the whole storytelling of the MCU to set this story pre-*Iron Man*. It was something that Kevin Feige had suggested. We thought that sounded awesome. I was in high school in the '90s so it has been a blast going back and looking at all the references, from the movie references to the music references. There is lots of '90s music in this movie, both good and bad. We had fun with that.

One of the challenges was that Nick Fury's role is so big in this movie so we had to de-age Samuel L. Jackson a little bit. He didn't need much – we ran some tests and the guy looks good.

Flying - by plane or by super power - plays a big part in this movie. What can audiences expect to see when Carol takes to the skies?
RF: Carol is a pilot, so there's going to be a lot of flying vessels and vehicles. By the end of the film, she'll be capable of flying on her own. ▶

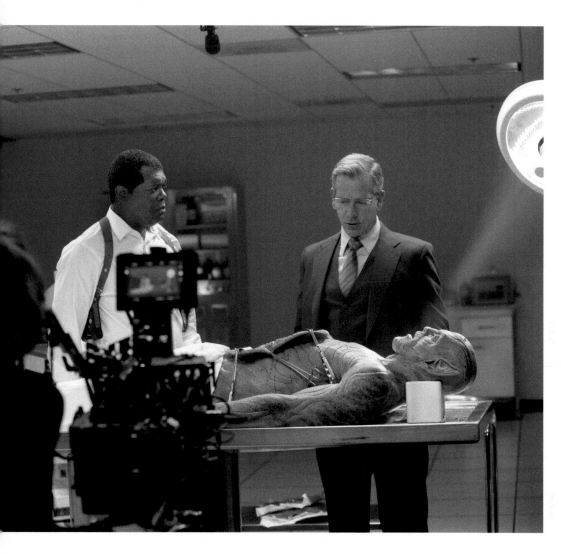

06 Brie Larson and Samuel L. Jackson team up as Carol Danvers and Nick Fury take cover

07 Nick Fury discovers we are not alone

08 Shooting with the co-operation of the US Airforce

09 Ronan the Accuser previously appeared in *Guardians of the Galaxy Vol. One*

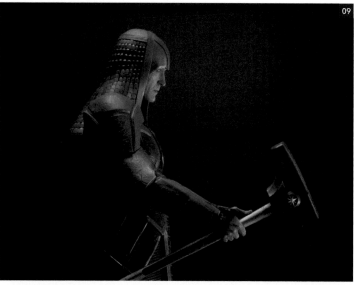

> ## "We love bad guys who have a certain kind of pizazz or charm to them, even when they are green, reptilian, shape-shifting Skrulls."
> *- Anna Boden*

▶ **AB:** Yeah, but she'll have to learn how to pilot her own body.

What role are the Skrulls playing in the movie?
AB: The Skrulls are shape-shifting villains, so there's this feeling that runs throughout the film that the bad guys could be anyone. A disguised Skrull could be your best friend, so this question of who can be trusted and this constant fear and paranoia is really fun to play with. We love bad guys who have a certain kind of pizzazz or charm to them, even when they are green reptilian, shape -shifting Skrulls.

How important is it to have the iconic Captain Marvel look?
AB: The suit is so great. She will also have a helmet that she will wear when she is flying in space, which looks cool.

What was the scariest aspect of working on this project?
RF: Anna and I have made movies that are really grounded and always on location, so one of the challenges was shooting with green and blue screens for the big outer space sequences. Luckily we're surrounded by people who've done this before. It was interesting to put those imaginative muscles to work in a way that we haven't before. ⊙

10 Brie Larson shows some swagger in her Captain Marvel suit

11 Anna Boden directs Jude Law and Lee Pace

12 Ryan Fleck works on a scene with Larson

13 Fleck and Boden flex their creative muscles on a night shoot

Kelly Sue DeConnick
Consultant

Kelly Sue DeConnick's run of Captain Marvel stories served as a direct inspiration for Marvel Studios' movie, leading to the acclaimed comic book writer consulting on the project...

01

Captain Marvel: The Official Movie Special: How cool was it for you to visit the *Captain Marvel* set?
Kelly Sue DeConnick: I make my living telling stories and using words, and I can't articulate what it was like! It was so fantastic.

When Marvel first announced it was making this movie, I was dumbfounded. I thought there was no way it was actually going to happen, quite honestly, and that if it did happen it would be huge and important. It feels silly to say important when you're talking about a comic book movie, but the message that this movie sends to little girls *is*.

What were your inspirations writing this character?
My dad was in the Air Force, so I grew up on Air Force bases. I pitched it as Carol Danvers as Chuck Yeager. It was about the metaphor of flight and really exploring the idea of escaping the fears and doubts we have about ourselves.

The really special thing about this movie is – yes – it's incredibly empowering for women and girls, but Marvel Studios hasn't made her a girl hero. It has let her just be a hero. It's great to be a woman, but sometimes men write women as though we don't have the same aspirations or the same fears or the same aggression. Carol's just *us*.

How has it been working with the filmmakers?
It has been incredible. I didn't even invent Carol – there are so many people involved, even on my run, like all the artists that I work with – Dexter Soy, David Lopez, Filipe Andrade, Emma Rios, Marcio Takara – who were co-

01 Brie Larson as Carol Danvers: an empowering hero

02 The Skrull march toward a confrontation with the Kree

03 Carol Danvers' Air Force career draws much from DeConnick's own experiences

> ## "To have been given the opportunity to consult on the film and to feel heard was cool."

You understand that somebody is going to undo your stitching, one day. I hoped something of my take would make it into the movie. Then to have been given the opportunity to consult on the film and to feel heard and have long, serious conversations about why the character works was cool.

Did you have conversations with Brie Larson?
When I visited her on set, I brought her some Beemans gum – pilots chew gum because oxygen dries out their mouths and sinuses, so they chew gum to keep moisture in their mouths.

It's great to talk to her, how could it not be? She's a phenomenal actress. It was important to me that Carol have a sense of humor. *Captain Marvel* is a very funny movie. The Marvel Cinematic Universe has captured the science fiction fun and the philosophy from the comics that if we all learn to work together we're going to win. I wanted Carol Danvers to feel like a grown up, and I wanted her to feel centered – and she brings that. ◯

creators on my stories. Before us, there were writers like Ryan Reed, Gerry Conway, and Chris Claremont who did incredible things with the character.

When you work in work-for-hire comics you have an understanding that even though you always want to write it like you own it, you don't own it. You don't want to get too attached because part of the joy of it is that the Marvel universe is the longest ongoing continuous narrative in human history, so to have been able to have sewn on that quilt is an incredible honor.

Brie Larson

Captain Marvel

Academy Award-winning actress
Brie Larson plays a noble Kree
warrior hero with a mysterious past.

Captain Marvel: The Official Movie Special: How did you prepare for the filming of Captain Marvel?

Brie Larson: I just tried to be as ready as possible. By the time we started shooting, I had been training for nine months. We started in January with three months of incredibly intensive training – because I really wanted to make sure that I could be clear-headed and prepared and know what I was doing. I'm so glad that I did.

On the first three days of shooting, I was on a moving train, and doing fight sequences, and flipping a stuntwoman – the amazing Heidi Moneymaker – over my head; doing kicks and punches up and down a train for three days: I felt alive. Everything I've done up until this point has been more cerebral, and to feel this connection to my body – in a way that I haven't felt before – is really exciting.

The *Captain Marvel* crew have somehow managed to be a kind of supergroup of all of my favorite crewmembers over the years. It has added to this beautiful feeling as if my whole life has built to this moment. I feel in awe of how special it is that we were all there together making this film.

Above all I feel a lot of tenderness, a lot of love, and a lot of respect over how many different experts and geniuses in different fields it took for us to make the movie.

> ## "Yes, there will be fight scenes and lots of colors and explosions; but there's gonna be real heart, and real moments, and finding the truth in all of this."

01 Captain Marvel makes her live-action movie debut

02 Carol Danvers takes some time to contemplate who she is

02 Blasting into action in pursuit of a Skrull aboard a fast-moving train

04 Carol Danvers races into action in her Kree uniform

It just requires a crazy amount of very specific talents. The costume was really hard to make. Some genius spent way too much time on this. You can't help but feel like saying "thank you" a lot!

What was it like working with Jude Law?
We trained together a little bit. I think we had a really good start, because [Directors] Ryan [Fleck] and Anna [Boden] and all of us on the performance side really care that we're not taking any cheap shots with this. Yes, there are fight scenes and lots of colors and explosions; but there's real heart, and real moments, and finding the truth in all of this. Finding the truth in space.

How does it feel to be joining the Marvel Cinematic Universe as Captain Marvel?
I think it became clearest to me once I was on the set of *Avengers: Endgame*, when I was looking around. [That was] day one for me. We were all doing a scene together, and I thought, "Oh, this is like the world's largest touring theater company." You feel the sense of gravitas that comes with being on a set like this, because there's an understanding that if this was just about spectacle and computer generated imagery, you don't need to hire me. You could hire anybody to do that. You're hiring us because of who we are as artists: because of our minds, because of what it is that plagues us, keeps us up at night, and what drives us.

That's all the stuff that ultimately goes back into these films. The car chases and the explosions are super fun, but, really, what sits with you, and makes you think, and makes you re-watch, are those interpersonal relationships and the conflicts between these characters.

Do you think that's something that started with Robert Downey Jr. and Jon Favreau in *Iron Man*?
Whether they realized it or not, they set it up from the very beginning. Downey Jr. was the wild card at the beginning of all of this – he was an unexpected choice at the time. I don't even know how old I was when that movie came ►

> "Marvel is at the high-stakes poker table betting it all every time, and somehow coming out on top every time, because it's doing what's honest."

out – I was quite young, and even I understood what was at stake there. So it made for this really dynamic, surprising performance. You were constantly surprised. And that's the way Marvel Studios continued.

Even seeing *Avengers: Infinity War,* every two seconds things were subverted. When you thought you were going to cry, you were laughing; when you thought you were going to laugh, you cried. You thought there was going to be an explosion, and it was a tiny moment; when you thought it was going to be a small moment, something big happened. They've done such a good job of keeping you on your toes that it's worth it to go see the film.

I've found that a lot of the time, especially when a lot of money is at stake, studios start to play it safe. They start to worry about the risk and want to try and make sure that they can protect their investment as much as possible. Whereas Marvel is at the high-stakes poker table betting it all every time, and somehow coming out on top every time, because it's doing what's honest. It really aligns with who I am: when I'm on set and I'm performing, I don't think so much about the specific choice that I'm making; I just think about what's available to me and what's honest in that moment. If it's true, then it can't be wrong.

Who is Carol Danvers?
What this is all about – and this is from the original *Captain Marvel* comic book – is that she is Kree and she's human – she's half and half.

The Kree are incredible warriors, hyper-intellectuals, the best at what they do, and also totally devoid of emotion. Then there's this other part of her: this human part that is the loving part of her. But it's also the part that makes her kind of sassy and a little brash at times. It makes her really emotional. It makes her aggressive and competitive. All of the good and all of the bad is in that human side. It's the flaw, and it's the best thing about her.

I think she's incredibly relatable in that way, because we all have two sides of our brains. We all have the left and the right brain. We have the logical, and we have the emotional. And we have the war of the two of them. Which one is of most value? Which one should we bring to the table? So that internal struggle is what makes playing her so interesting for me, because I'm basically playing two characters at once, and that keeps the movie constantly surprising.

It sounds like you really latched on to that conflict.
You have to think about what the potential future holds

05 Captain Marvel: she is Kree and she's human… She's incredibly relatable

for something like this, just like if I was doing a long run of a play performance. It has to be something that, as you grow in your life and as your life continues to evolve, there is something in this that will continue to inspire and intrigue you.

That's what any good piece of art – any book, movie, painting that I've ever seen – I grow with it. And as you grow, each time you reread the book, you're like, "Oh, I didn't even see it from that perspective." So, going back to the basics of the mentality of logic versus emotion, that will be a struggle within me for the rest of my life. l can continue to explore that forever.

Can you talk about the period in which this film takes place in relation to what has gone before?
It is interesting that we are going back, especially with the climax to *Infinity War*, where everything is at this major crisis, and I've been called in. Now we're going back to the very beginning, and seeing the origin of all of this. Even if you're not familiar with these films, I think that it will be a fun ride, but if you've watched all of them, if you're committed to this journey, I think you'll enjoy all of the little pieces that are the seeds of what's to come.

It seems like this was always the plan in order to give more weight to your character.
Yeah, I know, I don't really understand how they do it. It's a magical group of people making this happen. I totally agree with you: it seems like all of this was leading up to something in the same way that I feel like my entire lifetime of experience – being a woman along with all these other bizarre aspects of me – are all coming together to play this character right now at this period of time. And it couldn't have happened at any other time other than now.

Do you think this film will offer a new perspective on the Marvel Studios movies to date?
Yeah, it really changes the perspective. Once you know what she starts and what it inspires within the film, it changes the entire perspective of the rest of the catalogue in this very profound way that I'm purposefully trying to stay detached from because it's too big and too weird. And also I am not allowed to talk about it with anybody, so it's best if I just forget what I know, which is really cool and really big!

It's powerful stuff. Part of what made me feel the stir to do this was when Kevin [Feige] told me that his daughter hadn't seen any of the Marvel movies and that this would be the first one that she sees. That put things into perspective for me, understanding the potential of what this was and the timing of it.

▶ You worked with Samuel L. Jackson in *Unicorn Store Movie* and *Kong: Skull Island*. How does it feel to be reunited with him on *Captain Marvel*?

Sam's my family. We are the dynamic duo that the world didn't know it needed. This is our third film together, and we just love each other and have the best time together. I can talk to him about anything. He's just a masterclass actor – he's the greatest that there is – so I was so thrilled when I found out that he was going to be on this ride with me.

What is Carol Danvers and Nick Fury's relationship in this movie?

Carol and Nick do not start off on the same page at all. They're both at war and don't understand each other very much. But it's actually that conflict that brings out their sense of humor, which is the beginning of realizing, "Hmm, maybe you are like me…" And then they team up and are able to utilize both of their skills together. They complement each other very well.

You make it sound almost like a buddy movie.

Yeah, exactly. There are a lot of movies in this movie. But one movie in this movie is the buddy cop comedy.

Can you give us some background on the Skrulls, and how actor Ben Mendelsohn factors into them?

The Skrulls are shape-shifting aliens. They "sim" their host, but they can only sim recent memories, so they only have a short amount of info, which is how you can find out if they're a Skrull – because a Skrull could be anybody.

Ben Mendelsohn is one of our Skrulls, Talos. He's an incredible actor, so talented, so funny, and brings an Australian accent to a Skrull. I don't think anybody knew Skrulls were Australian, but they are! (Laughs) Ben's bringing that to the table.

What is Starforce?

Starforce is this elite group within the Kree army. We're like a special forces, and we all have a special set of skills. You've got guns, you've got swords, you've got fists, you've got rifles, you've got antigravity, and together we make this elite squad that is quite cohesive. They have a great familiarity with one another. They are brothers and sisters in arms.

But you do notice that Carol is a little bit of an outsider – because it just wouldn't be Carol unless she were an outsider. So there's a bit of a push and pull that you don't quite understand, but then it pays off later.

> "Once you know what she starts and what it inspires within the film, it changes the entire perspective of the rest of the catalogue in this very profound way."

FROM THE PAGES OF MARVEL COMICS...

Carol Danvers was created by writer Roy Thomas and artist Gene Colan. She made her debut in *Marvel Super-Heroes* #13 (March 1968) and later became the first version of Ms. Marvel in *Ms. Marvel* #1 (January, 1977) when an explosion fused her DNA with Kree warrior Mar-Vell, giving her superhuman powers.

Captain Marvel later joined forces with the Avengers and the X-Men. Carol Danvers has gone under numerous aliases during her career including Warbird, Binary, and Captain Marvel.

Does that outsider mentality play into the pilot side of Carol?

I guess so. Pilots are, for the most part, on their own. The thing that I found so unique in Carol from reading the comics and from the script and learning more about her, was that sense of humor mixed with hyper-intelligence and total capability in whatever challenge comes her way. I realized after going to the Air Force base that this is what Air Force pilots are like. So that spirit of her, the core of her, is the Air Force.

You did a lot of research into being a pilot. How did you find your experience in the air?

Oh, I puked a lot! I puked the whole time. That's part of how I got my call sign. All of the pilots were like, "You're not supposed to tell anybody that." And I was like, "I got no shame." I puked the entire time. We were simulating a dogfight, so I was flipping around all which way. It would be crazy if I didn't puke. We were on the offense, then we were on the defense. My pilot is so incredible,

super talented. We got to 6.5 Gs. It was amazing to feel all of that, especially once we were on set.

Just the other day we were simulating a barrel roll, and I was able to recall that exactly, what that feels like, what your body feels like, how hard it is to breathe. It's all of those little nuances that I hope will come through in the movie, so that regardless of who you are – if you're in the Air Force or you're a pilot or whatever – that you go, "Oh, I know that. I recognize that. That feels real."

How was your experience working with the directors, Ryan Fleck and Anna Boden?

It's been really wonderful working with them. They've worked so hard and diligently on the script in particular and crafting out this structure and story. I feel so grateful that they've given me the most dynamic character that I've ever had the chance to play. They come from the same world as I do – we both came from that scrappy indie film world – so to be with them on this feels surreal. ○

06 A behind the scenes shot of Brie Larson, poised for action

07 Ready for take-off! Larson poses on the *Captain Marvel* set

08 Ready to take flight. Larson's real life airtime adds a sense of realism

09 A Kree on a mission: Danvers navigates the 1990s

Samuel L. Jackson
Nick Fury

Samuel L. Jackson returns to the Marvel
Cinematic Universe as Nick Fury. However,
Captain Marvel's 1990s setting offers a
version of the character that has yet to
lose his hair and his eye, and is still to
embark on the long path toward becoming
Director of S.H.I.E.L.D. and creating
the Avengers Initiative...

Captain Marvel: The Official Movie Special: You've been a part of these films from the start. Has the enormous appeal of the Marvel Cinematic Universe surprised you at all?
Samuel L. Jackson: There are a lot of people that have been brought into the mythology of what all of this is – especially in terms of what the Marvel Cinematic Universe is – and it's still just scratching the surface of it, for people who spend time in comic book stores and everywhere else. They know there's a much bigger universe than the one that we explore. But they also know the mythology very well. It keeps the flow going in the social media world – people who argue about this, that, and the other, or what it means.

What's your take on Nick Fury's role in the origin story of Captain Marvel?
Being able to introduce the characters, being able to organize them, Nick Fury becomes what we know as a master manipulator. That's his superpower. He knows how to bring people together and manipulate them to get them to do what needs to be done to serve the greater good. It's been cool doing that, and introducing these characters, and showing different sides of them in terms of an audience watching them. In the one-dimensional world of comic books, the characters say things, and you have to interpret in your mind how they said it, and what they meant, and how they felt when they said it.

Marvel has figured out this very unique way of presenting characters in serious situations that are very exciting – dangerous – but still add the element of humor

that allows you to relax every now and then while you're sitting there watching it happen; to experience the fun of being a Super Hero who's in a dangerous situation as opposed to the fraught, inherent, tense grittiness of all of that. It gives you the adrenaline rush of danger with the mixture of a good laugh so you can relax for a minute while you're watching it.

How does it feel to play a character with such a long arc over so many films?
Actually, part of the challenge for *Captain Marvel* – being that I got two eyes, and it's almost 30 years ago – I have to forget who Nick Fury is at this particular juncture because he hasn't formed those opinions yet.
He's essentially a bureaucrat. He's still a badass, but he takes orders. He's one of those people that does not believe in extraterrestrials until he actually meets one, and even then, maybe we need a straightjacket for her…
I have to be reminded of that when I'm doing this particular film, that I'm not there yet. Nick Fury still has a light side that we don't see a lot of in those other movies. He has this weird, ordinary-person sense of humor.

Do you feel personally responsible for Nick Fury?
I do. Everybody comes in, and everybody has this idea of who we are and what we're doing, and sometimes we have to remind them that we've been in this playground for several movies. "You're the new kid in the playground, so watch us play and then make up your mind about how you want to get yourself into the game." Some directors get that. Some don't. It takes them a minute, then somebody

01 Samuel L. Jackson as Nick Fury, 1990s style

02 Jackson and Brie Larson share a joke on set

03 Fury joins Carol Danvers in the cockpit

04 Ready for take-off? Fury takes to the skies

FROM THE PAGES OF MARVEL COMICS...

Nick Fury was created by Jack Kirby and Stan Lee. He made his debut in *Sgt. Fury and his Howling Commandos* #1 (May 1963), a series set during World War II.

The character was later a CIA agent, first appearing in *Fantastic Four* #21 (December, 1963). Fury returned in *Strange Tales* #135 (Aug. 1965) as a spy, leading S.H.I.E.L.D. thanks to the Infinity Formula, a medication that kept him alive past his natural lifespan.

First appearing in 2001, the Ultimate Marvel version of Fury was based on Samuel L. Jackson, long before he was cast in the role. Marvel later replaced him with his African American son Nick Fury Jr., who is also inspired by Jackson.

from somewhere else will call them and go, "They know what they're doing, pay attention to them – they know the playbook. You're learning the playbook."

You watch *Black Panther*, and it feels like this unique and awesome thing that you've never seen before. But when you hash out the costumes and some of the political rhetoric that was allowed to be put in it, it's the same playbook, but it worked so well.

You can put all kinds of stories around it, so it never seems like the same story, but it plays out the same way. The excitement is there; the drama is there; the humor is in there. All those things come together. [The characters] always feel like people that you would like to hang out with: "I would love to be in that; I wish I was there."

There are all these things that Marvel has found a way to make an audience invest in, in a way that they've never invested in these things before. There's something about watching a Marvel movie or a Marvel hero that – if he's not super-duper crazy – anybody feels like they can put on an Iron Man suit and be Iron Man. Everybody's sitting there watching that and going, "I wish I had one of those suits; if I had one of those suits – wow, the things I could do."

Watching Bruce Banner trying to turn into the Hulk when he couldn't: it's like you sitting at home, and you feel yourself doing it a little bit, and you go, "Oh, he was almost there..." It's a very real thing, and it's funny,

> ## "Being able to introduce the characters, being able to organize them, Nick Fury becomes what we know as a master manipulator. That's his superpower."

and it's honest, and it's something that you can invest in: "I could see that; I could feel that; I could be that."

What do you think about the way Marvel Studios plays with genre?
When you look at the structure, it's like I was saying: the playbook is an interesting playbook because there are things that have to happen through the beginning, middle, and end. You start with a premise – it could be a heist movie, or it could be a "let's find this thing" movie. Or "there is a mysterious being doing something, let's figure out who that is" kind of movie.

With *Captain Marvel*, there is a buddy cop element to it with me and Carol. It almost develops a *Lethal Weapon* ▶

"With *Captain Marvel*, there is a buddy cop element to it with me and Carol."

05

▶ kind of thing. We meet, we're in an adversarial position. We don't have to have a knock-down drag-out fight to become buddies, but we have to come to a place where I understand something about her, and she understands something about me. There's a level of trust in that belief of who each person is, and helping that person discover something. She helps me discover things about myself, and I help her discover things about herself. In doing so, we bond in an interesting sort of way, because I understand that she has a level of humanity that she's lost touch with.

How does that figure into Nick's development?
There's a literal discovery of self in this movie. [Carol] literally doesn't know who she is. Nick helps her discover who she is, and in doing so, understands that what she is now and what she was before combine to give him an understanding of the universe that he didn't have before – that there is a way to find people who have extraordinary abilities that aren't a threat, that are people who will be helpful.

And on Carol's part?
Using her humanity gives Carol the strength to take on this superhuman thing that happens for her. That gives her a different understanding than any character in the Marvel Cinematic Universe about what it means to be a human being and what your responsibilities are, because you have this marvelous and larger-than-anything power. She literally is the most powerful individual in the Marvel Cinematic Universe. I guess people will come to see that. But she needs an understanding of her humanity to harness that and use it in the right way.

The level of acting talent in the Marvel Cinematic Universe is something to behold.
It's an awesome call sheet. When you look at the names that pass through here – Michael Douglas, Laurence Fishburne – it's crazy to try to think of everybody that's done it. The fact is [Marvel has found] a lot of actors who have done a lot of different things in terms of their theatrical careers and their cinematic careers that they can marry all these things together.

People often criticize something that they don't understand. When people start talking about dialogue in films, a lot of dialogue sounds stupid until you put it in the right people's mouths that know how to interpret it and bend a word here or bend a word there. But [Marvel has] found people who understand language in a specific way.

When you're working with somebody like Joss Whedon – Joss writes specific comic book language, and

05 Nick Fury and Carol Danvers both take a journey of self discovery

06 A Marvel Cinematic Universe veteran, Jackson offers a different take on Fury in *Captain Marvel*

07 Nick Fury shows his softer side as Goose gets some attention

if you change an "and" or a "the," he'll go, "No, just say it the way I wrote it." So you've got to figure out how to say it so it sounds like two people talking, or so it sounds like something that's emphatic, or something that's very meaningful that looks like something you would read in a comic book bubble – because you can't write monologues in those things.

I think Robert Downey Jr. brought a lot of respect to the character of Iron Man. Then, Marvel Studios brought me in. I don't profess to be all that, but I know the language of these movies and I know the intentions of the character. I know what is needed for each scene, what you want is somebody that understands that there's a fanciful nature to what's going on here, but what's happening right here is also very serious.

Everything's not funny to everybody. Most of the actors that they hire understand that there's a percentage of people that are going to laugh and there's a percentage of people that are going to sit there and go, "Huh?" – and there's a percentage of people that are going to laugh just because everybody else is laughing and get it later. But those actors have to understand that you don't have to hit that. You just lay it out there and let an audience get it.

different kinds of films. When you see them in the Marvel Cinematic Universe with a costume on, audiences are thinking, *What is he going to do with this? What is this guy going to bring?* Then they bring something special. I think that's been one of the huge differences between the success of this, and the lack of success of some other people's franchises.

What does Brie Larson bring to Captain Marvel?
What Brie brings to this is that level of respect of an audience that I'm talking about. She's done a very serious movie that she won an award for; she's done a very funny movie that people loved and laughed at; and she's been in an adventure story that I happened to be in with her where we're running from a big, hairy monster. But she also has this real-life thing that's very genuine for young women, and women in general, where she's a champion of women's rights. She's a believer in equality of standards for everybody to live by, and people respect her for that.

For her to become that person with superpowers is an amazing thing that's going to resonate with a whole bunch of young girls – mid-20s, and older women – because they know who she is. They take her seriously, and she takes what she does seriously. When they see her do this, it will be an enormous success for all of them as well as for her, and she takes that responsibility very seriously.

When I see her at work, I mess with her, and I try to make a joke. We've done three movies together now, and I love working with her. I love coming to work and talking to her. We laugh, but when we hit the playground, the games become serious. It's great to see her here. ○

Marvel Studios has been able to find actors that were willing to buy into what the character is. You take a guy like Benedict Cumberbatch: Doctor Strange is a very serious dude in the comic books, especially when you're reading the comic bubbles. But [Cumberbatch] knows how to deliver that stuff in a way that really connects with the audience.

I think it's very important for the genre itself to not take itself too seriously, but to give people a sense that these characters are genuine. In order to make that work for an audience, you have to hire actors that audiences respect in a way, or that they've spent their money to see before in

> **"Carol literally is the most powerful individual in the Marvel Cinematic Universe. But she needs an understanding of her humanity to harness that and use it in the right way."**

Ben Mendelsohn
Talos

A sinister warrior of the shape-shifting
Skrull race, Talos is portrayed by acclaimed
Australian actor Ben Mendelsohn.

Captain Marvel: The Official Movie Special: How did you first become involved with the Marvel Cinematic Universe?

Ben Mendelsohn: I wound up joining the Marvel Cinematic Universe thanks to *Captain Marvel*'s directors, Ryan Fleck and Anna Boden, who I'd made a film with called *Mississippi Grind*, about a couple of degenerate gamblers. Ryan and Anna were embarking on this film, and they very kindly asked me if I'd like to join the Marvel family.

Are you a comic book fan?
I'm a mild comic book guy. I had a period of reading comic books and whatnot, mainly Marvel titles.

Did you do any research for this role?
The script trumps anything else. But I was aware of Skrulls, and I was aware of the Kree.

Can you give an overview of the Skrulls?
The Skrulls are basically these tough, lizard-looking aliens that are big and aggressive. They can do something that makes them very formidable indeed. If I was Skrulling – which I'm not, by the way – but if I were, I could sit here and look at you, and in a minute, I could *be* you. Think of it like a chameleon ability, but amped up; because the other thing Skrulls can do is, they can get inside your little human mind. This makes Skrulls very formidable because of their camouflage ability which, combined with their strength, means they can really rumble with the Kree. The Kree basically look like they're friendly eco-warriors in comparison!

What's your take on the Skrulls?
The Skrulls are like the heavy metal rock stars of Marvel, as far as I'm concerned. They're like AC/DC. They're direct. They're three chords. They rock.

What do the Skrulls want?
The Skrulls are in the middle of a war with the Kree, and it's not going well at all. The die-hard Marvel fans will know exactly what I'm talking about. The Skrulls have intercepted the Kree warrior Carol Danvers and have looked into her mind in order to try and understand their enemy.

What did you like most about the script for this film?
What's beautiful about the way the script is written, and what's beautiful about what we're capturing, is that Ryan and Anna are really flipping a lot of ideas on their head. They're also making this great hero's journey of Carol Danvers' story. I'm pretty proud to be a part of it. Marvel Studios has basically gotten better and better at what it does.

Marvel Studios certainly don't rest on its laurels or play it safe…
I think it's testament to the confidence within that studio. It has just gotten really good at it. People are gonna find out stuff in this film that they didn't know about Nick Fury. Things like, "Where did he get his eyepatch?" There's a lot of information in this film that people will assume that they know, or people will assume they know what's going on. There's an enjoyment to the way that [the filmmakers have] been approaching things. They do swing for the fences; they want to hear that crack, and they know how to get a home run. So, there'll be a lot of things that people will find out – not least of which is the velocity it takes to break through a roof on your way to Earth!

Do you find it at all strange that the film's setting, the 1990s, is now considered a period piece?
I'm afraid that's the truth. We've gotten there – the 1990s are now an antique proposition. There were things in the '90s that we can do now that they couldn't do then and vice versa. It's a great period of history though. It's a lot of fun to go back there, because we are stepping back in time. We show what Nick Fury was like 20-odd years ago. I think people will have a lot of fun going back in time with us. ▶

01 Ben Mendelsohn as a disguised Talos

02 The actor had previously worked with directors Ryan Fleck and Anna Boden on *Mississippi Grind*

03 Looks familiar? Talos examines a Skrull corpse

04 *Captain Marvel* marks the first appearance of the Skrulls and their leader, Talos, in the MCU

> "There'll be a lot of things that people will find out - not least of which is the velocity it takes to break through a roof on your way to Earth."

03

04

▶ Were you excited to be part of such a great cast?
It's an esteemed company of actors. Let's start at the top with the Captain herself. Brie is an incredibly formidable dramatic actor, she's a fantastic comic, and she is so physically strong. I don't think I'd want to try to go toe to toe against Brie. I think she could do some serious damage if she wanted to!

Samuel L. Jackson – I mean, wow. He's one of the most enjoyable actors to watch. When you go and watch something that he's in, you just know that you are going to have a good time. I mean, he's Samuel L. Jackson!

Then we have the mighty Jude Law! Jude's an excellent human being and a fantastic actor. Annette Bening is a great actor. So, it's a good squad.

How have you found working with the blend of practical and digital effects on this film?
I whack on the Skrull head – we know we're going Skrulling! – and then I chuck on the costume, and I go on set. I look around – look, there's Captain Marvel! Ooh, that's Nick Fury over there! Everyone's there, everyone's in situ. People should maybe stay away from green screen unless they're amazingly good at it. Marvel knows how to use it where it's supposed to be used.

What do you think have been the strengths of the Marvel Cinematic Universe?
I think that from whatever those guys were cooking up at the start – Jon Favreau and Robert Downey Jr. – that was a smart move, because it's interesting. If you know anything about Tony Stark, you know he's a man that had difficult times in the comics. This is the thing about Marvel: the comics were grittier than the other titles at that time. They were more tangible. They were more human. They spoke

FROM THE PAGES OF MARVEL COMICS...

Talos was created by Peter David and Gary Frank and made his debut in *The Incredible Hulk* (issue 418, 1994).

Born without the ability to shape-shift, usually a common trait of the Skrulls, he made up for this deficiency by becoming one of the most feared Skrull warriors within the Empire, earning the title Talos the Untamed.

05 The Skrull have landed! Talos and his troops come down to Earth

06 Mendelsohn gets Skrulling!

07 Talos plots his next move against the Kree

to social and personal issues in a way that the other titles didn't as much. But that was just a stroke of genius, and I think it set the bar high.

You know what? I didn't expect *Iron Man* to be a great film. *Iron Man* is a great film. They did a great job. There's a joy about it. I think that's a pretty good bar to aim for.

Of course, Marvel Studios has done some great stuff since then. *Thor: Ragnarok* was just awesome. The best of the films, for my money, have a certain joy in them in the way that they carry themselves and the way that they go about their business.

Black Panther is a pretty emotional film, and it's beautifully played. It's played with a great deal of dignity and a great deal of swagger at times, and a lot of poignancy. They're not things that people necessarily would've been comfortable marrying to comic strip ideas, but they're things which fit really well. I think it says more about the maturity with which people can now approach the original source material – which is the comic book –

> ## "I imagine there will be a serious amount of fan discussion about what's going on."

as a genuine work of art.

For the longest time, comic books suffered from this faux highbrow tut-tutting. I think that stuff's got a long tail to it. You think about the old gods – the tales of the great path, and the Nordic gods, and I'm sure many other cultures. Such is the world of the comic book, in a way. There are these ongoing tales about these enormously powerful creatures that deal with our dilemmas. It's a really satisfying experience to watch these stories unfold. ○

Djimon Hounsou
Korath

Having previously appeared in *Guardians of the Galaxy*, Djimon Hounsou returns to the Marvel Cinematic Universe as the Kree soldier, Korath.

Captain Marvel: The Official Movie Special: How does it feel to be back in the Marvel Cinematic Universe?

Djimon Hounsou: Oh, it feels great to be back in the Marvel Cinematic Universe. They're creating a world for everybody to exist in, in a way. My character Korath, from *Guardians of the Galaxy*, exists despite having died in that movie. He has a life, has a backstory in *Captain Marvel*, so, for my character, this is almost like a backstory coming to life.

After Korath's demise in *Guardians of the Galaxy*, did you think he might return?

No, the way things ended up last time on *Guardians of the Galaxy*, I wasn't so much concerned about whether he would be back or not. I view my character as one of those unstoppable machines that, even once you feel like he's been terminated, he comes back. You can reanimate him again!

Is it fun to be back in the MCU?

Yes, I think it's fun. It's great to be able to recreate some of the backstory in *Captain Marvel* – where he came from before and all that. Certainly, it is fun to be back.

Where do we find Korath in this movie?

At this point, he's one of the members of Starforce, the elite force of Kree soldiers. We get to see him much younger, and more dynamic.

What is Starforce's aim?

Starforce is trying to restore peace.

Was it interesting to see how the Kree operate culturally?

It's a little more defined as to my character within the Kree world. In *Guardians of the Galaxy*, we discover him, and that was that, but the thing that's cool about this story – all these Super Hero films – is they slowly create and invent this world in which you happen to exist, as the collage of those stories comes together. When you look at Nick Fury, he's all over the place. In that sense, you get to create a world in which we Super Heroes truly exist.

How does it feel when you put on your costume?

With any Marvel Studio film, the costume is a character in itself. A costume that looks great is sometimes not necessarily fun to wear, but they look visually stunning. During the fitting processes, it would be nice to remember that you have to use the restroom from time to time!

How helpful do you find it to shoot practically?

It's a little helpful. The nature of some of these films is that there is a lot of green screen, and a world which does not really exist. Most of us are left with the imagination of a director or visual effects people. The only time we really get to appreciate this is at the end of the film when it's nicely put together. It certainly is sometimes a bit of a challenge to know what you're looking at. We try to imagine the world and that setting and make it believable.

> **"I view my character as one of those unstoppable machines that, even once you feel like he's been terminated, he comes back."**

01 Kree warrior Korath poised to strike

02 A deadly serious warrior, Korath is the butt of Carol Danvers' joke

03 The armor maketh the Kree - a battle-ready Korath

What is Korath's relationship to Carol?

It would seem like it's one of those relationships where Carol tends to make lots of jokes at Korath's expense. Korath is somewhat one-dimensional; he doesn't smile too much, he's just a straight-on killer; he's a hunter.

Do you think *Captain Marvel* will inspire audiences to go back and look at the previous Marvel Cinematic Universe movies in a different way?

Oh yes. I think Marvel Studios has created a world of its own, and a very interesting world. How they complement one another; how those characters that are reappearing evolved – certainly Nick Fury, who appears everywhere and somewhat seems to be dictating the pace of these stories. Kevin Feige has a very full mind with so many of those ideas.

03

Would you agree that character development is as important as action sequences at Marvel Studios?

Yes. You have all the explosions and all the wonderfully choreographed fights, but at the end of the day, you still need to keep a certain organic nature of those characters. All those characters need to feel human – all apart from my character!

How have you found the fight choreography?

I'm focused on my choreography, but because of the limitations that I have with the costume, all the things that you have trained and rehearsed to do, you get there on the day of filming and you realize you can't really spin around and throw a punch like you normally would, because you're so restricted under the costume. So the action is limited to one or two moves, basically.

Some of the actors had a bit of padding under the costume, on the shoulders and rib cage. My costume does not have any padding. We went into the desert, Simi Valley, and I had to run with my gun drawn. That sand was like a powdery type of sand, and on my first step, it was like running into quicksand. I lost my footing and went over, head first.

It's very challenging to be doing action sequences with the costumes; but without the costumes, none of us are Super Heroes really.

Can you tell us a little about the Kree's relationship to the Supreme Intelligence?

We all belong to the Supreme Intelligence – that's how we get our orders. Certainly, that's the way we communicate with the Supreme Intelligence, and where we also get regenerated.

What's been your experience with the rest of the *Captain Marvel* cast?

We have a tremendous cast on this film. Brie Larson keeps us somewhat grounded. It's great to see Samuel L. Jackson again. We have the amazing Jude Law. There are some great actors that came in just for a short time on the film – Lee Pace [Ronan, who also appeared in *Guardians of the Galaxy*] worked on the movie briefly – so it's an amazing ensemble cast.

Marvel Studios has been described by some as the world's biggest repertory company...

It's fun how Marvel is approaching bringing all those characters together. It's quite rare to have a story in which you can really have, and embellish, a cast like this and not miss out on the story. A lot of times, when we tell any normal, regular story with such a tremendous cast list, the focus tends to be on the cast and not so much the story. ○

Algenis Pérez Soto
Att-Lass

Originally hailing from the Dominican Republic, Algenis Pérez Soto made his acting debut in 2008's *Sugar,* directed by Anna Boden and Ryan Fleck. *Captain Marvel* sees him reunited with the directing team on a very different kind of movie.

Captain Marvel: The Official Movie Special: How does it feel to be a part of the Marvel Cinematic Universe?

It's amazing to be a part of this Marvel family and to be one of these Marvel characters. It's awesome to be working with Anna and Ryan, the directors of the film, and all these actors that I used to see on TV – Oscar winners, Oscar nominees. It's a great experience for me.

What do Anna and Ryan bring to this project?

They bring the reality, because as directors they are coming from independent films. I happened to work with them before on one of their films. They can add their reality to this amazing film, their vision, plus all the action. I think it's a great combination.

As part of your research for your character, did you look at any of the Marvel comic books?

I've always been a comics fan, and I know many of these characters. When they told me the character I was going to play, I went back and started reading about him – what skills he has – and using the script and what I found out about this character, I had an idea of how I was going to approach it. Then when the directors tell you exactly what they want, it's a mixed idea. Once you can see every point of view of these characters, you can start working with that.

Which aspects of Att-Lass most appeal to you?

His relationship with Carol Danvers – I really like that part of his life. He looks up to her as a big sister. I really like the sense of closeness that they have in the film.

01 Att-Lass: A Kree master of infiltration

02 Taking his place in the squad

03 Att-Lass takes aim at the Skrulls

> ## "Att-Lass is very sleek; he's very fast; he's got his two blasters, and he's very skillful with those."

What can you tell us about Starforce?

They are very skillful warriors who are sent on missions, and are commanded by Yon-Rogg. The cast is amazing. To have all these members of the Starforce, like Jude Law, Brie Larson, Gemma Chan, Rune Temte, Djimon Hounsou – it's really cool. I've really enjoyed working with these guys on all the sequences that we have together.

What does Att-Lass bring to the group?

Everybody in Starforce has their special skills. Att-Lass is very sleek; he's very fast; he's got his two blasters, and he's very skillful with those. On a mission, if there's somebody that needs to go unnoticed on an infiltration mission, that would be Att-Lass.

How does your costume and the makeup inform your character?

I don't know exactly what it is, but when you get the suit on and your makeup, you feel like a Kree. When I have my costume on, and I have the guns in my hands, I feel like I really have these powers this guy is supposed to have. The suit can be a little uncomfortable at first, but once you get used to it you just want to have it on all the time! I love it!

How have you found working with the visual effects?

Before I even had an idea I was going to be in a Marvel Studios movie, I used to look on YouTube to see how they film all these movies – to see the amount of green screen and all the effects that they use – and wonder how the actors feel when they are pretending they are looking at something and they don't have anything in front of them. I always wanted to do that, and now I have the opportunity, and at the same time the challenge. When I step into one of the ships, or I'm supposed to be looking at something in front of me when I know there's nothing there, I have to use my imagination as to how things are supposed to be.

How much prep did you have to do for your fight scenes?

It's a lot of work, but it's fun to do. I was talking to my stunt guy, and I was telling him, "Throw whatever ideas you have at me to make this character look really cool; I want this character to look badass; I want him to look like he's really good with his guns and the way he fights."

Has the way Att-Lass fights informed your performance at all?

When I first read about the character, and then when I was talking to my stunt trainer, we were discussing who

exactly this guy is. He's very fast with his guns, and he's very aware of not just his situation but his teammates' situations. He's paying attention to whatever he's doing, but at the same time he's turning around and helping his friend. It's really cool.

What do you think audiences will take away from the character of Captain Marvel?
With this character, Carol Danvers, Brie is representing women, I think. In this movie she's representing how powerful women can be. She's going to be one of the strongest characters in the Marvel Cinematic Universe, and that's going to be really inspiring for women. Also, when

she finds out that she had a life on Earth, and people get to see that, there's going to be a nice twist that people are really going to love and enjoy about this character.

Do you think Captain Marvel will cause audiences to reassess the previous Marvel Cinematic Universe movies, in terms of what they thought they knew?
I think it's going to be fun for a lot of people, because it's going to make them go back and see what's happening in the other movies, and then realize where all these characters are coming from. That's going to keep everybody on their toes as to what's happening in this movie. That's going to be really interesting.

Is there anything in particular that you personally are looking forward to seeing in the finished film?
Honestly, I want to see the whole product, because I haven't been in all the scenes. I can't wait to see some of the fights that we've had as a group – there are going to be a lot of effects, and the choreography, the skills, all these guys fighting alongside you, everybody doing their thing. It's going to be really cool! ○

FROM THE PAGES OF MARVEL COMICS...

Created by Mark Gruenwald and Mike Manley, Att-Lass AKA Captain Atlas, first appeared in Quasar #9 (April, 1990).

Att-Lass fought the Avengers and the Shi'ar, but on learning that the war was orchestrated by the Supreme Intelligence in order to further the Kree, he became disillusioned. He was killed when he deliberately activated his battle suit's self-destruct.

> "When you get the suit on and your makeup, you feel like a Kree."

Lashana Lynch

Maria
Rambeau

Lashana Lynch plays one of Carol Danvers'
oldest friends - a fellow Air Force pilot who
goes by the call sign "Photon."

Captain Marvel: The Official Movie Special: How does it feel to be part of the Marvel Cinematic Universe in *Captain Marvel*?
Lashana Lynch: I've been a big fan of the movies for a very long time. I watch them with my friends and we have big discussions afterward. I've been aiming to be a part of the MCU for at least two years. So, now that this has happened, it's like being a tourist in a place that I know!

What got you most excited about getting to be a part of *Captain Marvel*?
I was really excited that Marvel Studios was focusing on it's first female Super Hero – the most powerful Super Hero, I might add! The studio is giving Captain Marvel a chance to shine –– and we are getting to see her journey from the very beginning, and maybe in years to come we will see the end. As a fan, that's beautiful to be a part of. She is the first female Marvel Super Hero to have her own film and we also have our first Marvel Studios female director. You see the first black, female, single mother in the Marvel Cinematic Universe. There are female writers, female crewmembers – there are so many females everywhere and it is undeniably a feminist film. We have come so far along in the industry and it feels like there are many people that are still a step behind. Marvel is right where it needs to be.

01 Ace fighter pilot Maria Rambeau

02 A skilled pilot in a male-oriented world

03 Rambeau follows her friend on a mission to the stars

04 A close friend of Carol Danvers, Rambeau is shocked when her friend returns, seemingly from the dead

05 Lynch was pleased to bring her experience on gritty dramas to the film

How risky is it to set this movie in the '90s?
That's exactly why Marvel Studios is so great, because it takes the big swings at things. It just keeps everything so consistently sparky – every single time it's something new. I know what happens in the comic, but I don't necessarily know for a fact what's going to happen in the movie, and that's exciting. I think that's why fans are so glued to it, because they know Marvel Studios is representing the comics and then some. That's what we look for in filmmaking, that we're going to represent everyone in their own light and know that there's going to be a chance where everyone potentially gets their own film. It may or may not happen – but it keeps us on our toes. That's great for an audience member.

Are you a comic book fan?
I chose not to read the *Captain Marvel* comics until the day we wrapped this movie because I'm playing Maria Rambeau, who is featured in the storyline of Monica Rambeau, her daughter, in the comics. It's exciting to take someone new on board and to characterize someone who's never been seen before. For me, it was better to create someone new and fresh and really take that privilege on board of being able to build a character that no one's going to compare to anyone else. Whatever choices I come up with for Maria is what she's going to be –– and that's really exciting.

And this is the 1990s, before anyone has heard of the Avengers.
Because no-one's ever seen the Avengers before, Maria doesn't believe in aliens, whereas Monica in the comics is quite fascinated with all of that. Maria learns that her friend Carol is a part of it, and Carol was full-on human just a few years ago.

What is Maria and Monica's relationship to Carol?
Maria Rambeau is an amazing former fighter pilot. She is someone who was capable of many, many things in her occupation but didn't necessarily get to fly. She is from a male-orientated environment. Carol and her are stuck together like glue. They were so tight when Maria went on to have Monica, Carol naturally became an aunt to Monica, and they were like a little family, going in and out of each other's houses. Wherever they moved around the world, as you do when you're in the military, Carol was there being her backbone. So then when Carol died, her whole world was shattered. Maria could only draw on the strength of having been a fighter pilot before and having Monica to keep Carol alive in a way, in their memories. So, when Carol just decides to swing on by to her house, the way she deals with that is quite beautiful. She comes straight in with the sarcasm. It's like their relationship is exactly the same,

03

04

05

> ## "Carol has been through this whole experience that Maria doesn't understand and doesn't take quite lightly or easily. She will do anything for this woman."

and she's ready to just give her that shorthand and be that person that reminds Carol who she is.

She's been through this whole experience that Maria doesn't understand and doesn't take quite lightly or easily. She will do anything for this woman. That's why she risks her life and leaves her child and goes into space, because she knows she could trust Carol with every fiber of her being. It's beautiful to see that the relationship that we have, the closeness, the sisterhood, the love, and the fact that it has been them against the world.

Marvel is a giant action machine with rich characters...
I think that's why *Captain Marvel*'s going to be so special, because there are so many little parts of the movie that are like little independent movies. And it's great to have Ryan Fleck and Anna Boden because they come from that ▶

FROM THE PAGES OF MARVEL COMICS...

Created by Roger Stern, Maria Rambeau's daughter, Monica, took the mantle of Captain Marvel and eventually became a member - and eventually leader - of the Avengers for a short period.

She became known as Photon for a while and is now known as Spectrum.

06

background. They're bringing such a niche, artistic, artsy, particular, but very free flowing experience to Marvel. It feels like we have the best of both worlds in *Captain Marvel*. A lot of the actors in this movie are from an independent background. I'm from a kind of kitchen sink drama background. Brie is from a similar background where she did films like *Room* that had very small casts and a lot less make-up!

It's nice to all come together with our different experiences and make this very balanced, very fleshed out story. You do something really special where it's just you and another person having a conversation and having that moment to breathe because, with a lot of Super Hero movies, you don't often get the chance to breathe through moments. And with this, we're getting the exact time we need to show what every character means and show who they are from the beginning in order for us to see where they're going to grow towards.

Whjat can you tell us about the cast?
I have been a big fan of Brie's for a long time. I think she's amazing. Every single person I meet, I say, "Oh, by the way, just so you know for your personal knowledge, Brie's amazing." Samuel L. Jackson has been great to get to know. It's been very good to do this first Marvel Studios

06 Larson and Lynch contribute to fleshing out the story

07 Sharing a joke with the amazing Brie Larson

> ## "It's nice to all come together with our different experiences and make this very balanced story."

movie with him, because he's practically done all of them! He knows exactly what he's talking about. And he knows how to maneuver around this set like water.

Ben Mendelsohn is amazing and hilarious to work with. He's so lovely, so dedicated, so sweet, and really caring. Also he's not American, so, sometimes when I'm talking to an American and then I'm talking to an Australian person I start to think, *Where's my accent again? Who am I?* Gemma Chan and Djimon Hounsou are actors who I've watched for years. I remember seeing Djimon at Soho House and thinking, *Oh, gosh, I love that guy. I don't want to say anything. He's doing his thing. I'm just going to leave him alone.* And then a year later we're doing a movie together. I love how this industry works and how you can just cross paths with everyone and really witness the talents that they have in such a different way, because maybe you're used to seeing someone in a drama. And now you see them being a Super Hero. ◐

Jude Law
<u>Yon-Rogg</u>

British actor Jude Law makes his Marvel Cinematic Universe debut as Yon-Rogg, an inspirational Kree warrior driven by a belief in the divine leadership of his people.

Captain Marvel: The Official Movie Special: How did it feel to join the Marvel Cinematic Universe as Yon-Rogg?

Jude Law: It was like being invited to a party. For the last few years, I'd heard about who has been at the party and I know some of those people and greatly admire them. I'm a fan, so being able to step into this world and live in the world is thrilling.

What have directors Anna Boden and Ryan Fleck brought to the movie?
Anna and Ryan bring a humanity, a morality, and a sense of humor. There's a wit and smartness to the storytelling and it's a complex story. Following the reiterations of the scripts and the rewrites of the order of the story was really interesting.

Anna and Ryan have got a great sense of storytelling and rhythm, which has been worked on so that it really delivers. The story reveals its secrets in just the right order at just the right time. Within this vast world, with these epic battles and alien races, there is a heartfelt and human story, which is what will reel you in.

Why was *Captain Marvel* a good project for your entrance into the MCU?
I think it was an amalgam of things. I think there was a sense of relish at how fresh these last few Marvel Studios movies felt. I liked the way they were reinventing themselves and how the filmmakers were drawing humor out of them.

Anna and Ryan had a great take on the Marvel material, and I admire Brie Larson. I thought Brie was a fantastic piece of casting for the role of Vers.

Who is Yon-Rogg?
Yon-Rogg is the commander of Starforce, which is an elite special forces division of the Kree army. He is also a mentor to Vers. He found her in a very early confrontation, which led to her becoming super powered. He brought her back to life with Kree blood and she has been his pet project. He feels responsible for guiding and containing her skill sets, honing her abilities, and trying to keep her mind from drifting into more human, emotional places, and becoming therefore more focused, driven, and less emotional, which is more of a Kree and certainly more Star-force's way of doing things. They have a tight bond, but Vers' humanity still comes out, and I think that is hugely attractive to Yon-Rogg. I think he finds her irresistible, and it's her human elements that he really warms to. ▶

01 Jude Law as Yon-Rogg, leader of Starforce

02 A military commander, Yon-Rogg is Starforce's finest

03 Training with his protégé, Vers

04 Yon-Rogg and Ronan: dedicated followers of the Supreme Intelligence

05 Two Kree warriors who share a unique bond

> "Yon-Rogg brought Vers back to life with Kree blood and she has been his pet project. He feels responsible for guiding and containing her skill sets..."

FROM THE PAGES OF MARVEL COMICS...

Created by Stan Lee and Gene Colan, the Kree military commander Yon-Rogg made his comic book debut in *Marvel Super Heroes* #12 (December, 1967).

A highly trained soldier Yon-Rogg has super-strength, agility, and stamina, and is highly-skilled in numerous forms of unarmed combat.

05

▶ Did you do much research into your role?

I was a comic book reader when I was younger, but for a very short period of time. For this film, I wanted a quick education into the storyline that inspired the movie and these characters. Marvel sent me some comic books to read, and then I relied on the script and treated the role just as I would any other piece of work.

In the film, what are the Kree trying to accomplish?

The Kree are a warring nation fighting the Skrulls, who they see as their greatest threat. *Captain Marvel* is really a film about conflict and propaganda. The Kree are a very dominant and very aggressive race, or at least their military and their leaders conduct themselves as such.

Marvel Studios tackles social issues which are rich and fertile areas to dip into. The stories feel relevant and political in many ways. They are stories of empowerment, of introspection, of learning to confront your ills and your dark side. I think that is why these movies are so popular with audiences.

How is it that Marvel Studios has been able to cast such great actors?

Actors are drawn to certain projects; they want to be in things that people see. They want to be in films that are popular and want to be in safe hands so that they know that their work is being well treated and that they look great! That's how you get the best out of performers, so, of course, Marvel Studios is able to draw the top end. As soon as you hear that Brie Larson and Samuel L. Jackson are at the center of the piece, it becomes a project you want to be part of. You know you're in good company.

What's it been like working with Brie?

I feel that acting is like playing tennis; you want to play against someone who can raise your game. I arrived to work on the film with a couple of months to train up and learn the fight choreography, and she'd already been there for three months. Her dedication to the part is extraordinary. She has really led from the front, and she always arrives on set in great spirits and really well-prepared and is fun to be around. ▶

> "The Kree are a warring nation, fighting the Skrulls, who they see as their greatest threat. *Captain Marvel* is really a film about conflict and propaganda."

"As soon as you hear that Brie Larson and Samuel L. Jackson are at the center of the piece, it becomes a project you want to be part of."

How did you build the chemistry with the other members of Starforce?
We were fortunate in that we had quite a bit of time before the shoot began where we were in each other's lives and rehearsing. So there was an opportunity there to get to know each other and establish a very natural dynamic, which I put down to really good casting. Each person brought a different quality to the group as a whole.

It helps when everyone's incredibly approachable and friendly and fun, and that was the case on this film. We all slotted very quickly into our roles, both as we were making the film and in front of camera.

We became a unit, because we were always together, whether it was at the early hours of the morning coming in to work or sharing our grievances about our suits rubbing or getting too hot! There's nothing like that to bond a group of people.

Do you find that putting on the costume transforms you?
Absolutely – a costume always does that anyway. I'm always astounded at the power of seeing myself for the first time in a costume. It gives me such assistance in finding my character and performing as that character. We had several costume fittings and the attention to detail and the quality of the suits the costume department made are just extraordinary.

How do practical sets enhance the performance?
The CG really is embellishment – certain sets are fully constructed. Once the sets have been lit by our brilliant cinematographer, Ben Davis, they look like an alien world.

What do you hope *Captain Marvel* brings to the MCU?
I think the origin of S.H.I.E.L.D. is wonderfully satisfying – how they start out as bright-eyed ingenues not really knowing that this other world of heroes exists. I think having a character as powerful as Captain Marvel on the good side is really exciting, and the fact that she has a fantastic sense of female strength and intelligence is really unique to this character and particularly to this film.

Have you ever worked with so much smoke before?
Smoke and dust, they were the two ingredients. I've had a very interesting experience with my nose on this film! Things were coming out of my nose that I've never seen before. That happens after four days in a dust bowl with smoke in the air. Oh, I'm a big, tough Kree! ◑

09

Annette Bening

A highly acclaimed actress, Annette Bening faces an unusual challenge as she makes her Marvel Cinematic Universe debut..

01

01 Award-winning actress Annette Bening joins the Marvel Cinematic Universe

02 As well as amazing special effects, Bening applauds the movie's focus on people

03 Galactic war has befallen the Kree

Captain Marvel: The Official Movie Special: How did you become involved with *Captain Marvel* and the Marvel Cinematic Universe?
Annette Bening: I'm very lucky that I got to be in this movie. I had no idea that I would ever get to do something like this. Marvel Studios came to me, and said, "Hey, we're making this movie – Would you think about being in it?" I said, "Really? What's the story?" So, they showed me the story, which I needed a little bit of prompting on, like, "Okay, who's the good guy? And who's the bad guy?" Then I met with the directors, Anna Boden and Ryan Fleck, and they talked to me about what they were envisioning.

Do you think setting the movie in the 1990s was a risky move on Marvel Studios' part?
We have this fabulous female character who goes through the hero's journey, from confusion and trying to figure out who she is, to owning her own power. That's the classic hero's journey.
The references and the music and the technology

> **"The storytellers are taking certain established premises of the Marvel Universe and subverting them."**

of the 1990s seem like another time now. Of course, to some of us it's not another time, it's just real life! Like, when [Carol] crashes to Earth, she crashes into a Blockbuster video store.

I think that one of the things that Marvel has been able to do is find really great stories and great directors who are focused on story, like Anna and Ryan. Even though we have a lot of special effects it's still all about the people. It's about real human feelings, and growth, and challenge, and change, and adversity. How do people deal with adversity? And what is it that gets us to our true, authentic selves? This is really what the story is about and that's fun to see.

There's humor in these movies, which is so key – music and humor and character. Whether it's an animatronic character or whether it's a real person, I admire the way that they're approaching the casting of these characters – like Robert Downey Jr. I was talking to my son about it the other day. He was like, "Remember when we saw *Iron Man*, and it was so awesome?" And he remembered when he was a kid, and what that was [like].

There's a part of us that wants to get in touch with that part of ourselves no matter how old we are – that sense of fun and adventure. We're reassured that the universe is a complicated place, but in the end, there's a meaning to it. There's a meaning to adversity, and there's a place that we can get to, like Captain Marvel does, where she realizes that her own power lies in discovering her own true, authentic self.

How have you found the shooting of the movie, working both practically and with the visual effects?
It's a human story. That's why they hired Anna Boden and Ryan Fleck – they look at it as a human story – and Brie Larson, a great actress who's going to question and want to make sense of it on very simple, human terms. That's how they approached me with it, and that's the only way I know how to approach things.

So even when we walk into this awesome virtual chamber set that's quite surreal, we're still just talking about, what am I doing to a certain character? What are they doing to me? What's the challenge? How does this fit into the story? In the end it's really about that. The technology and the visual effects and the virtual reality of it all serve that basic human story about wants, and needs, and what's in the way of what I want. What am I trying to get to? What am I doing to get it? And that is really what the story ends up being about – human challenges.

What was it like working with Brie Larson?
That's the part of it that is fun: interacting with these really talented people that are very down to earth. In the end, you're in front of the camera, you're working opposite somebody, and it's that feeling that comes between you. Most of my scenes are with Brie, and I get to watch Brie – I get to see how she's dealing with what she's got to do and the questions she's asking. And she insists that it's real for her and that it's grounded in the story and the journey of the story.

Sometimes, of course, within a scene you have to break things up into little bits and pieces to shoot it. That's where the talent comes in. You have to have the ability to ignore any distractions around you, such as green screen, and find a way to just let all that go. You have to let your performance be the personal and human journey that you're trying to embody. That's what it's all about – with humor.

For me, the really fun Marvel movies are so good because of that humor and the sarcasm at times. It's not earnest – that's not any fun. All the characters have a certain kind of swagger and joie, and that's certainly true of *Captain Marvel*. ○

Gemma Chan
Minn-Erva

The London-born actress takes the role of sharp-shooting Kree soldier, Minn-Erva, who establishes a rivalry with new recruit Vers.

02

"[Minn-Erva] was Yon-Rogg's favorite, so there's a little bit of a playful rivalry when Vers arrives on the scene."

What can you tell us about Starforce?

The Kree society is a very structured, quite militaristic society. They value their warriors above anyone else. The Starforce are elite warriors, so their status in society is very high. The other thing is the Kree have been engaged in a long war with the Skrulls, who are their mortal enemies.

When I spoke to Anna and Ryan, we talked a lot about trying to get into the mindset of the Kree and why they do what they do. For me, it's: "This is us. That's them." You put the Kree first before everything. There's a real pride in that.

The Marvel Cinematic Universe feels like a universe of fully-formed characters; is that something that's been carried through into *Captain Marvel*?

Yeah; it's amazing how you can juggle all these characters, but yet each one is memorable. I think that's what Marvel Studios does really well. You want the audience to be interested in the nuances of every character, even if you only see them for a couple of scenes – you could easily go off and explore that route or that character. It's a fun dynamic between Starforce; every character is different.

The other interesting thing to say is that every character communes with the Supreme Intelligence before they go into battle. It's a very private thing that a Kree will see when they're connected to the Supreme Intelligence, so it was interesting to think what each individual member saw. That's a big part of their preparation and their motivation.

How did you research for this role? Did you read any of the original comics?

You can do it in different ways. The script is very much its own thing; it's a new interpretation and adaptation of the story and those original characters. I think that's a nice thing actually; it means that even if you're familiar with the comics, you're not going to be quite sure what to expect when you watch the movie.

As an actor, it's fun to look up the origin of the character, but you take it with a pinch of salt. You've got to just look at the script that you've got in front of you and really work on how you're going to tell that version of the story. I've done a little bit of research, but Minn-Erva in this story is quite different to who she was in the comics. In the comics she was a geneticist, while I'm a sniper in this story.

What about the Kree? Did you research their history?

I know Ronan was in *Guardians of the Galaxy*, and he appears in our film, because our film is set before that. So I had an idea that maybe he wasn't the nicest guy in the

C aptain Marvel: The Official Movie Special: How did you become part of the Marvel Cinematic Universe?

Gemma Chan: I got a call from my agent, as you usually do; they said there's an audition, but it's all top secret, so I didn't know what project it was for. I went on tape in London and sent that off into the ether, and thought, "Well, I probably won't hear anything back." Then I heard that the directors wanted to Skype with me, so I had a Skype session with Anna Boden and Ryan Fleck, and then I taped another scene. Then they offered me the part.

Were you given much information about your part and the movie?

Marvel Studios can give you limited information, but obviously you're not allowed to read a script. [The directors] can tell you what they've got as an idea for your character, but you've really got to put your trust and your faith in them. But the track record is great, so I didn't mind too much about that.

Tell us about your character.

I play Minn-Erva; she is a member of the Starforce team. She's Kree – she has blue skin, some blue hair. She's pretty badass; she's the team's star sniper – and until Vers signed up with the team she was the star. She was Yon-Rogg's favorite, so there's a little bit of a playful rivalry when Vers arrives on the scene.

01 Gemma Chan as Minn-Erva

02 Minn-Erva and Att-Lass don their Kree armor

03 Minn-Erva and Bron-Char take a break from the action

04 Taking aim at the Skrulls!

MCU. But within the dynamic of the Starforce team, you get to see another side of them being quite playful. There's a warmth within the team.

How do you feel about the film being set in the 1990s?
That's really exciting. It will be interesting to really watch the movies that come after *Captain Marvel*, knowing what people will find out in this film – how Fury became Fury, and Coulson's introduction to this world. It breathes new life into everything. It all plays with people's expectations or assumptions about the Marvel Cinematic Universe.

Also, the '90s is just such a great time period. We're now far enough away from it that we look back and you're reminded of things – like Blockbuster Video – which we all used to have and don't exist any more. I love the way they've weaved those references into the film.

What are your thoughts on the rest of the *Captain Marvel* cast, and the wider MCU cast?
I was over the moon when I found out who else was going to be in this film. Brie is fantastic. Annette Bening is a legend; I still get a bit tongue-tied around her – trying not to blurt out that I love her whenever I see her. Ben Mendelsohn is fantastic; Jude is fantastic; and then you've got people like Lashana Lynch, who's amazing too.

It's a privilege to work with such great actors, and then to know you're also joining this wider company of actors who are brilliant. We come together from all over the world, from many different backgrounds, to tell these stories. It's exciting.

How have you found working with the visual effects?
I've actually been surprised at how little pure green screen we've done. They've built some incredible sets; most of the spaceships are sets that have been built. We've done scenes

on location up by Shaver Lake and in Simi Valley, and, again, they've built some sets into the landscape. So, really, it's not been that much green screen, at least for me. There's all this '80s and '90s memorabilia on set; there's a pinball machine there, and there's a jukebox – it's great.

What about your costume? How has that been?
I'm in a very cool, quite restrictive costume, so, when I'm in it, I have to hold yourself a certain way. I can't slouch in it because the costume won't let me, and I can't lift my arms too high. It looks great, but it is quite restrictive.

Minn-Erva also has a mask, which she wears when she's on a mission. We've had a few battles in the mask, the mask and I! I couldn't see out of the original mask that I was given, so at one point the team had a blind sniper. But we've fixed that – it all came together. ●

FROM THE PAGES OF MARVEL COMICS...

Radically different from her movie counterpart, Doctor Minerva made her debut in *Captain Marvel* #50 (May 1977), The creation of writer Scott Edelman and artist Al Milgrom, Doctor Minerva is a Kree geneticist and enemy of Mar-Vell. She later became the partner of fellow Kree Captain Atlas.

Rune Temte
Bron-Char

A former star football player for Norwegian team Strømsgodset Toppfotball, Rune Temte takes on the role of Kree soldier, Bron-Char.

Captain Marvel: The Official Movie Special: How does it feel to be a part of the Marvel Cinematic Universe?

Rune Temte: This is a dream come true. It's a whole universe, and it's a universe of so many things. Seeing Marvel come from the comic book world, and how it has grown into the Cinematic Universe, and to now actually be a part of it, has been an amazing experience. To my knowledge, I'm the first Norwegian to enter this fantastic franchise and universe. There's a Dane in *Doctor Strange* – Mads Mikkelsen – so there's a second Scandinavian, but to my knowledge I'm the first Norwegian.

When I first came in I was really impressed with all these talented people, some of whom I know have been working on nearly all the movies. It's obvious to me that Marvel has found a formula: keep getting the good people back, and keep the knowledge and everything within the system. It really shines through. Like today, I came into the makeup trailer, and you can see they know what's been going on. You can sense it. I've been around for a while now – not on the big movies like this, but I've been doing a lot of work over the years – and you can feel the energy, that people know what's going on.

What can you tell us about the Kree?

They've been around forever, and they've always protected their race. There's always fighting with the Skrulls – these wars have been going on and on and on. Obviously they are an alien race – they are more than human – but maybe we can relate to them in some form. As you see in this movie, they are different shapes and different colors even. We are warriors, and we protect the Supreme Intelligence.

It's quite interesting with the Kree that the best things, the best characterizations from all the people, are gathered in this Supreme Intelligence, and they all feed from that. So, when our hero arrives, she is actually a product of that. That's why she is the most important, the strongest Super Hero in this universe.

How did you approach the role of Bron-Char?

I landed on three words for this character: raw, real, and beautiful. That was what I went for. Of course, you have the camera, you have all the settings, you have to be within the frame; but as Ingmar Bergman said, "Within the frame is your limit, but within the frame you are totally free."

With this character, there are no boundaries. For an actor, this is fantastic. Anna Boden and Ryan Fleck are very talented and generous people; they will say, "We'll have this; we don't want this, but we'll keep it." Then you

01 The formidable Kree soldier, Bron-Char

02 Bron-Char in consultation with comrades

03 Bron-Char in the heat of battle

04 A key member of Yon-Rogg's squad, Bron-Char is a seasoned warrior

can throw in things. This confidence is very important for an actor, that they will allow you to come with something that's coming from you.

Bron-Char is the leading protector of the Supreme Intelligence, even though he's maybe third in command in our group. He's a fighter, and I hope it comes through in the movie that he really enjoys his fighting and takes it seriously. This is his life, and when you think of someone being a fighter, it's going to color how they move, how they interact. So that was what I was trying to bring to the table this time.

Presumably a big part of that is the character's physicality…

I really enjoy this kind of work; it's basically using everything you've got, moving. I used to be a professional athlete, so using my body in different ways is fantastic – and this character, he can move. He's a big guy, but he can shift, he can jump, he can run. We've been doing some fantastic stunts.

Is it important to you that you do as many of the stunts yourself as possible?

It's good to look back and say I actually did it. We do whole choreographed fights, and when you're playing a warrior

"This character, he can move. He's a big guy, but he can shift, he can jump, he can run. We've been doing some great stunts."

character, it's part of the whole thing: how you move, how you do these things. For obvious reasons, I can't do it all, and we leave it to the people that can take care of it. But I like it. I think it's fun.

Doubtless your costume helped with you finding your character, but were there any personal touches that you brought yourself?

They were thinking of cutting my beard at one stage. I didn't want to get too much involved, because you're sort of a newcomer, but I actually sent an email. I said, "I think it's a good idea to keep the beard because it's part of my personality now, and it brings out a little bit of what the Kree have been before." I was really pleased they left it; it brings out those Nordic features that I have.

How have you found working with the rest of the cast on this film?

I very seldom get starstruck these days, but I did when I met Samuel L. Jackson. This is an actor that knows his craft; this is someone that carries a lot of weight. Of course, he's the nicest guy there is. When you look at this cast, when you look at the movies they've done – and the iconic movies he's done – I find it's very inspiring to work with people that bring so much into their work. It sparks off all of us.

Brie Larson: the way she carries herself as a person, as an actor in this setting and on a big movie like this is really impressive. As the lead on this movie, she deals with a lot – it gives me hope that she is so personable with everyone on set. As a newcomer coming in, it's very important that you meet this warmth and this welcoming, because even though, as you get older, you've been around, you've done a few things, it's still a new project. You know they know their craft, so it's very inspiring for me.

Djimon Hounsou has had the experience of being a Kree before, in *Guardians of the Galaxy*, so that was really nice. He shared his experiences with me. I've followed his work, and he has a fantastic presence. Also, they're bringing young talent into this Starforce group. I'm very pleased to work with all of them and feel the energy in the group, since I'm a lot about what really goes on between people and what you can get out of this group.

What was your initial experience on joining the *Captain Marvel* cast?

The casting on the Marvel Studios movies has always been fantastic. Sarah Finn, the casting director, has done them all. Just to be considered in such a capacity has given me a lot of confidence that someone will see your talent if you have the endurance and you have the patience and you have the willpower. As you say over here, luck is when preparation meets opportunity.

I remember seeing a teaching video with Sarah Finn, and she was talking about how she wanted to see behind the actors' eyes. I find that really interesting that she thinks in that way, and she's willing to go through all that to find the right kind of people that will bring that something special to a part, something that is completely unique and distinctive.

04

What do Anna and Ryan bring to the movie?

From day one, you see immediately that they know how to give the actors the right information to get what they want, and at the same time give us freedom to contribute to the project. There's a lot of stuff going on and things are very visual, so you need that connection between the characters. From the work Anna and Ryan have done before, this is the kind of thing they do.

Also, a great thing with them is that they are so experienced with directing, writing scripts, and putting great stories and projects together, and so finding that dramatic line that you need to get something on the big screen. You can see the confidence and the experience they have. I think they have a great eye; it seems to me they have a vision. Also, they're great fun – that helps. They're very, very kind, lovely, empathic people, and you need that to have people bring their best work. It's fascinating to see directors like that work, because it's a big movie – a big project. It's a franchise.

What can audiences expect from this movie?

It will be engaging; it will be overwhelming; it will be entertaining; it will be surprising; it will be a joyride that will pull you from the first sequence to the last, and it's going to be spiced up with a lot of humor. ◉

Clark Gregg
Phil
Coulson

Clark Gregg has been playing Agent Phil Coulson since 2008's *Iron Man* in movies and on TV. His appearance in *Captain Marvel* takes the character back in time to the mid-1990s.

C aptain Marvel: The Official Movie Special: What's your perspective on these 10 years of Marvel Studios movies?

Clark Gregg: I remember seeing that Jon Favreau was directing this version of Marvel Studios' *Iron Man*, and then I saw that Robert Downey Jr. was going to play him, and I thought, *Oh, my God, that's perfect. That's incredible.* Then he got Jeff Bridges and Gwyneth [Paltrow], and I knew that Marvel itself was taking over the making of this movie, and, just because I had a lot of *Iron Man* comics when I was a kid, I was excited.

I got this call saying there's a little part in the movie that I might be right for. It's this guy, an agent; it's two scenes – a couple of lines. I was like, "Oh, I want to do that." But then I saw that cast and went, "Oh, they're going to cut me out, or I'm going to just be in the background of one shot, and everyone will say, 'Was that you in that movie?'" This had happened to me before, and I didn't want to do another film like that. My wife was like, "Shut up, you love this, go do it, they won't cut you out!"

Then I got there, and it was the most fun, and Jon goes, "They're going to add some more stuff for you. There's something about this guy they like."

That was 10 years ago, and I never thought the name "Phil Coulson" would become such a big deal in my life, or that I would get stopped on the street by all manner of humans who have some kind of connection to him!

It's been an amazing ride, as a fan of Marvel and as a fan of comic books in general, to see Kevin [Feige] and Louis [Esposito] and everyone at Marvel just knock it out of the park so reliably. Every time I thought, *Oh, we're going to do Thor, that's cool – they're going to let me be in Thor; but it seems a little trickier to pull off the Norse god who swings his hammer, versus the billionaire with the flying suit.* Then that was funny and amazing.

People ask me if I think audiences will ever get sick of Super Hero movies. Well, if they're just that narrow thing, perhaps; I think they might have. But so much of what Marvel has done has been innovative in terms of having it be one story. You're going to see the next chapter of a giant book that you're invested in, using really amazing actors and great filmmakers – and the films are really very funny, too.

Now we've got *Captain Marvel* where the Super Hero is a woman, and I get to take my daughter to see it.

01 Phil Coulson embarks on a journey that will change his life forever

02 The son of Coul, as Thor would call him (*The Avengers*)

03 Investigating the mysterious hammer in the prelude to *Thor* (*Iron Man 2*)

04 He may have been killed in *The Avengers*, but Agent Coulson lives! (*The Avengers*)

> "So much of what Marvel has done has been innovative in terms of having it be one story. You're going to see the next chapter of a giant book that you're invested in."

Coulson does seem to have become one of the constants of the Marvel Cinematic Universe...
To a certain extent, I may be the expert on Phil Coulson. But one of the really fun parts about it is, there's always been a certain license to let me play a little bit generously. I really believe the reason the character exists and the reason I have this gig is probably because Favreau was so generous, but also because Robert brought a specific kind of fun-loving, improvisatory style that I didn't even know I was going to love that much. The character and the dynamic was very much born out of that. So, I have him to thank more than anybody.

But also, it's a chain letter. Everybody adds a little piece. Zack Stentz and Don Payne and so many amazing writers took over and started adding great stuff for Coulson that all became a part of the canon – Thor calling him "Son of Coul" – and Joss [Whedon] taking him to the next step and turning him into this guy who cannot speak around Captain America and has been collecting his comics all his life. It does

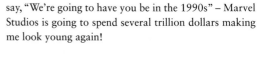

> "I never thought the name Phil Coulson would become such a big deal in my life, or that I would get stopped on the street by all manner of humans who have some kind of connection to him."

kind of feel like a family or a gang... I would say for life, but it's even apparently in the afterlife. I mean, I thought I was dead after the first *Avengers* movie, but I'm back doing another film.

How have the Marvel Studios movies formed such a consistent universe with such disparate characters?
It speaks of the strength of the concept that you get invested in this overall story, and you can then take real leaps. You can go out and meet Rocket; you can go deal with magic because you know that [the films are] chapters, and that somehow these filmmakers and the people at Marvel are going to find a way to make it all connect so you can put them all in the Avengers, and it feels like it works. You can put them all in *Avengers: Infinity War*, and that seems like it works, and so Thanos works. I think the same thing is true in *Captain Marvel*, which, turns back the clock 25 years.

This [movie] has also come along at this moment because the technology is evolving so much that they can

say, "We're going to have you be in the 1990s" – Marvel Studios is going to spend several trillion dollars making me look young again!

Taking that setting into account, is there a risk in doing this particular film?
Yeah, there's a risk in doing this. And there was a risk in the way *Infinity War* ended. That's really gutsy. It's one of the great act breaks ever written, and yet they did that. Now, well, you better tell a story that happens 20 years ago, because until [*Avengers: Endgame*] comes out, you can't make anything else in the present day without it being a spoiler of some kind, so it opens doorways as well, creatively.

How has it been working with the directors Anna Boden and Ryan Fleck?
I often [thought] while shooting this movie – as Coulson says in *Iron Man* – "It's not my first rodeo, Mr. Stark." I've seen time and time again directors who didn't have a huge background in this kind of movie being brought into the Marvel Cinematic Universe, and there's so much about the machinery here that gives them a chance to really thrive. They hired Jon [Favreau] – who I don't think at that point had ever made a movie like *Iron Man* – and backed him up when he was determined to cast Robert Downey Jr.. But also there's a commonality. When we were making the first *Thor* movie, Kenneth Branagh was tremendously fun to work with and brought a Shakespearian touch to it all, but also he was looking for the comedy, and brought a lot of enthusiasm.

I feel the same thing is true of Ryan and Anna. They have this intense enthusiasm for the material and a desire to honor what's been set up about these characters, and also take it somewhere new.

What do you think the audience's reaction to *Captain Marvel* is going to be?
I suspect they're going to walk in and have a nostalgic feeling around some of the '90s jams they're going to hear, and seeing some young S.H.I.E.L.D. agents in their '90s suits. They're going to think it's a stripped-down, smaller-scale origin story – and, boy, are they going to be in for a big surprise... ◦

Behind the scenes

A special section looking at how the Production Design, Stunts, and Costumes teams helped bring Marvel Studios' newest Super Hero to life...

Drew Petrotta and
Lauri Gaffin

Production Design

Members of *Captain Marvel*'s
Production Design team reveal
how they helped create Kree
weaponry, the recreation of a
Blockbuster Video store... and
stuffed cats!

01

Captain Marvel: The Official Movie Special: What kind of weapons did you create for Starforce?

Drew Petrotta: The leader of Starforce wears these gravity gauntlets that open up when they are activated. They help him control gravity, so he can pick up his enemies and throw them around. Like all Kree soldiers, he carries a pistol that he connects with a dagger to make one weapon.

Korath is a swordmaster who carries two swords, and when activated they become space swords. They're edgeless swords that can do a lot of damage.

Our sniper, Minn-Erva, carries this rifle and has a slightly smaller pistol because it fits her frame a little better.

How did you contrast this with the design for the Skrulls?
DP: In Kree design, everything is very angular, straight, and strict with no soft edges.

This is in opposition to the Skrull, which are very organic in their design. The Skrull rifle is finished in a purple ceramic. They also use a pistol and some less-than-lethal weapons. They have a "shock stick" and a stun rifle.

What was your biggest challenge?
DP: There are quite a few, actually. I don't know if anyone has succeeded yet in edge-lighting a sword and making it usable. This is the first sword I know of that's just lit on the edge. The actor can control when it's on and off, which took some doing. The lighting of the rifles and pistols was a little difficult.

It was a lot more difficult to create the Skrull world, mostly in finding a good finish that complemented what the production designer, Andy Nichols, had in mind for the world – where everything is ceramic and organic. Their costumes are very purple, so it was a pretty tough job finding something in that world that matched with the costumes and had a similar finish to their ships, and adding lighting to it.

Who builds the props?
DP: On this movie we used a vendor here in Los Angeles called StudioArt & Technology. They have made a lot of the props for many of the Marvel Studios movies. They have a lot of great ideas, some really good technicians, and they

> "In Kree design, everything is very angular, straight, and strict, with no soft edges."

always find a way to make this work out the easiest way for us. We find it's much simpler that way than opening our own shop.

What was your involvement with Goose, the cat?
DP: There are several cats used in the movie. We hired two very good cat wranglers and they brought a number of cats that all did different skills. I've never seen cats that are able to do the things that they did!

Then the visual effects team at Legacy Effects made a stand-in stuffed cat that was used for quite a few things. The resemblance to the actual cats was uncanny! It was really hard to tell the difference between the two when you're looking at them from across the room.

We had to use a fake cat for stunts and as a lighting reference during stunts when we didn't want to get an actual cat in any danger!

How closely did you work with the directors?
DP: I was very involved with them. My process started with

"For three months, we collected VHS tapes and made a Blockbuster label for each box!"

the production design. The art department had already developed space ships for the opposing forces.

I then had an artist draw prototypes of things and went and sat down with Anna Boden and Ryan Fleck and discussed our ideas. We made prototypes and showed them for sizing and shape, and did some color samples. Anna and Ryan were involved in every part of that process.

How challenging was it having a lead who is so physical?
DP: She is one of the most dedicated actors I've been around. She trained extremely hard with our stunt team. The stunt team and I came up with rubberized weapons that held up and wouldn't flop around, that were safe enough to deal with. For me, it was more dealing with the stunt team and knowing that she had trained to a level where she could replicate exactly the motions that needed to be made. I wasn't too concerned for her safety with our props because I knew her movements would be correct.

How difficult was it to make Blockbuster as authentic as possible?
Lauri Gaffin: This was our set for a crash scene. It took a long time to pull it together and make it very authentic. It's supposed to be 1995, so for three months we collected VHS tapes from all over the city and made a Blockbuster label for each box. We have 7,000 of them!

Then we sorted through them all and made sure they were before 1995. We had old ones, new ones, and children's ones. We replicated the original Blockbuster counter and then all the candies, which were a very important part of going to Blockbuster!

05

Are there any Easter eggs in this scene?
LG: We really wanted to make sure we had *The Right Stuff*. That was a film we wanted to get, and we actually bought those videotapes because they were very hard to find. When Carol Danvers creates an explosion, she blows the standee for *True Lies* through the window.

What other challenges did you face on the film?
LG: We set up a fair for the Massachusetts State Fair scene with a go-kart track in Ventura, California to evoke 1978. The challenge here was to create and find period pieces that would evoke the time, along with the appropriate props and wardrobe.

We brought in pieces from a company that holds carnivals called Candyland. They were able to supply period pieces, such as a Ferris wheel, a popcorn machine, and things that didn't use lots of LED lights and contemporary graphics.

I really wanted to use tents that were made out of canvas because it's right for the period. However, we had severe rains in California so we used plastic coated tents, which at least had the same feeling because they were the striped carnival tents.

In this film, our challenge was mixing the different time periods: 1978, 1985, 1995 with outer space and different universes. We have the earthly world but also the challenge of creating a feeling that you're in another time and place.

Do you take inspiration from any other Marvel films?
LG: Each film has to be different and have a new universe and planets. You don't want to have any reference to the other films except for the characters. ◗

01 Captain Marvel takes a journey through time and space – and the Production Design team helped convey that journey

02 Skrull sets were organic in design

03 No cats were harmed during the making of *Captain Marvel*!

04 On location for Maria Rambeau's house

05 Carol Danvers in an authentic 1990s bar

Walter Garcia and Hank Amos

Stunts

Walter Garcia served as fight coordinator on *Captain Marvel*, making sure battles had maximum impact, while second unit stunt coordinator Hank Amos made sure the practical action sequences packed in all the thrills Marvel Studios audiences expect!

02

Captain Marvel: The Official Movie Special: Can you talk about the fight between Brie Larson and Jude Law?

Walter Garcia: We have an awesome fight sequence between Brie Larson and Jude Law. Both actors trained really hard for this sequence. It features Yon-Rogg against Vers, and is a training sequence. It has a mentor-versus-student type of vibe, with a lot of fun bits for them to play off of each other. It's not just a gritty fight, but it's something that shows their relationship as a student and teacher.

The fight has acrobatic elements and we get to see a bit of Vers' abilities as she's growing into her new super powers.

How did Brie take to the intensive training the role demanded?

WG: Brie is the most diligent person that I've worked with. She puts dedicated time and effort into her training like no other person. She trained for two hours, five days a week, working on a combination of boxing, kick-boxing, Judo, wrestling, and some Jiu-Jitsu to prepare herself for this role.

How was training Jude Law?

WG: Jude got word on the street that Brie was training like an animal, so he arrived for his first day of training, and Brie had her boxing gloves on. I was holding the mitts for her. He got intimidated and scared, but it was the best thing for him because after that he started coming in for training every day. Their chemistry when they were doing the choreography was seamless; it really felt as if they had been training with each other for years.

What was your favorite day on the job?

Hank Amos: My best day on this shoot was when they shut down the city streets of Los Angeles and crashed a bunch of cars! We set up the final beat of the car chase where Fury purposely swerves over and does a T-bone with the bus. Amazingly, it went great – we just pulled it off.

Does it take a lot of preparation to arrange a big action sequence like that?

HA: People don't realize how much time it takes. It's a very challenging sequence, so when the audience watches this in a movie theater, I just want them to appreciate the fact that what they've witnessed on the screen is a culmination of so many talented departments. Marvel

01 Yon-Rogg and Vers go toe-to-toe

02 The fight shows the results of meticulous preparation by the actors involved

03 Vers takes on the Skrulls in a skilfully choreographed fight scene

04 A complex flight sequence

05 Carol Danvers takes to the skies, in a more traditional fashion

"Brie and Jude's chemistry when they were doing the choreography was seamless..."
- Walter Garcia

03

04

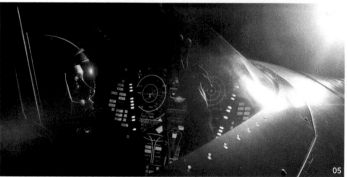

05

> ## "People don't realize how much time [a big action sequence] takes... It's a culmination of so many talented departments."
> ### - Hank Amos

Studios has a knack for bringing in the very best people from every department all around the planet. We have the very best special effects guys, the very best second unit director, the best camera operators, and the best stunt drivers in the business.

Is it important that stunts are practical?

HA: This movie is a real throwback. I would never knock our friends in the visual effects department, but sometimes it's easy to hand off the action to a computer. What they told us at the beginning of this show was that they wanted to do as much of the action as practically as possible. That is basically a license for us to go bananas – and we have! We've trained the ▶

▶ actors up to do all their own fights. When you see them flying through the air they're actually on huge rigs doing all their own flying.

All of the car-driving you see in this movie is practical. There are no computer generated cars. We get to take it back to the old school and do it for real.

Brie Larson seems to have really embraced the training needed for the part.
HA: Let me tell you something about Brie: We cannot kick her out of the stunt gym! We're saying, "Brie, we want to

---

"We cannot kick [Brie] out of the stunt gym!"
- Hank Amos

---

go home. It's getting late!" She's asking to do one more rep, one more pass, one more routine. It's been such a blessing to be working with an actress who is so dedicated and so committed. She was with us training for two and a half months before we even rolled the first bit of film – and that's unheard of. I hope audiences really appreciate her hard work when they see her on screen. It takes months of hard work, training and dedication to be Captain Marvel.

Is preparation for a chase very important?
HA: Yes. It's crazy because we're all over the town. When you see it in the film, it'll seem like we've just gone a few streets here and there. But we've utilized all the amazing scenery of Los Angeles, which means it takes us to different locations on different days. So, we have to move the whole circus every day and pull off these amazing stunts in a new environment. It's really challenging, but it's also really fun because it never gets stale.

What was involved in the sequence in which Carol Danvers crashes back to Earth?
HA: We have a scene in which Carol enters the Earth's atmosphere and comes back to Earth. She has her hero moment where she flies in and lands.

We utilized all of our stunt riggers and our best stunt doubles to make this sequence really work. It's one of my favorite types of stunt to do because it really requires the teamwork of five different people on five different lines to fly her in and have a smooth landing.

What sort of preparation went into this scene?
HA: It's a very tricky situation because we were out in the middle of nowhere using very heavy equipment. We had to do a lot of testing. Our tests for each stunt have to start from scratch because every stunt is different. There's really no science behind a stunt sequence until we are on

06 Behind the scenes as Brie Larson is rigged for a climb

07 The wires are digitally removed

08

09

the location. You always need to see what you're dealing with, and so we just have to go through all the steps. Step one is establishing how high we want her to be off the ground. Once we know that, step two is looking at how far back we want her to fly in from.

So, when we have our A and B together we end up with C, which is a really cool landing.

Do you have to take weather conditions – like the wind – into account?
HA: Of course. Wind and atmospheric conditions can really come into play when you're dealing with wirework, especially when we have got our stunt person 40 feet off the ground. When a breeze kicks up they might start to sway a little bit, so we have to be very careful.

Do you prefer doing stunts on location?
HA: This is my favorite way to do stunts. We had the most amazing backdrop of Lucerne Valley to work with, and we had the whole entire team working on one specific stunt. We utilized all of our resources with the heavy equipment and our winches and generators, and were able to create a magic moment right out here in the middle of the desert! ◗

08 A crash on the streets of Los Angeles took much planning by the dedicated stunt team

09 Action on the train as a high-powered sequence is shot, the first to be completed on the film

Sanja Hays
Costume
Designer

Sanja Hays has provided costumes spanning from the 1970s to the furthest reaches of space for *Captain Marvel*.

02

C*aptain Marvel: The Official Movie Special:* How did you initially approach the costumes on this movie?

Sanja Hays: *Captain Marvel* is pre-dating most of the other Marvel films, so in a sense it gave us a little bit more freedom. However, freedom is not always the best thing. There was not much to catch on to; the only thing we had was Captain Marvel and her costume. So it gave us a little bit of freedom, and a responsibility in doing the origin story.

At the same time, it is the Marvel Cinematic Universe, so there are rules that have been established that we had to follow – and there are comics, and people know the comics. Before I started, I looked through and read hundreds and hundreds of pages of existing comics.

How did you set about translating the costumes from the comics pages?

Designing for characters from comics is complicated, and challenging, and fun. A lot of the comics were drawn a couple of decades ago, so it is really just an inspiration. I looked through hundreds of pages, just to get into that world.

For the other characters, we looked for Kree people and for Skrulls and all of that, but at the end of the day it was mostly the colors and the feeling of them. We couldn't put Skrulls in purple spandex suits and black underwear. It's more about trying to be true to the idea of them, rather than the specific design.

Were there iconic elements you really had to incorporate?

For Captain Marvel, there were two things that were obviously iconic: the starburst sign and the whole chest piece is iconic, and then, of course, the red and blue colors. That was something that we couldn't deviate from. There was also another thought, which was a little different to some of the comics: she was going to be much more of a tomboy, much more of a pilot, so that it's believable that she is an actual hero and a soldier and a pilot.

Tell us about the construction of Captain Marvel's costume. Translating the sketches into real costumes that the actor

03

> ## "Designing for characters from comics is complicated, and challenging, and fun."

> ## "For Captain Marvel, there were two things that were obviously iconic: the starburst sign, and then, of course, the red and blue colors."

can wear can be challenging, because they have to not only be able to walk in them, they need to be able to perform actions. There were a lot of things that we had to take into account, like the right colors – which you can't get in every material – and it needed to be stretchy so that she can move every which way and perform the actions.

There were a few different versions of the suit. One of them is just the beauty suit. Another is one where she can sit – that had a shorter top part. Then when she's flying, we had soft shoulders, because all the hard parts of the costumes – like the chest, the shoulders, the gauntlets, the belt – have been sculpted and molded in a material that is bendable, but essentially hard. So when she lifts her arms or hangs, we have soft shoulders, and then where she needed to wear a harness, the suits had to be made bigger.

For some of the suits, the main fabric was leather. It was a special finish that's a little bit pearlized in blue, so that it has a sheen in the light. Some parts are made out of glideskin, which is essentially a neoprene that is a little bit shiny. We had to over-dye the color because it's way ▶

01 A fully suited Vers complete with her signature mohawk!

02 Carol Danvers keeps a low profile

03 The iconic Captain Marvel costume

04 Vers in her Kree battle suit

05 Carol Danvers in functional flight suit

▶ more stretchy, but we couldn't make the whole suit out of that because it breaks in a strange way. So, it's a lot of little things that you have to look at.

We had seven or eight suits for Brie and her two stunt doubles, but if you look at her costumes, you would never know which one is an action costume and which one is her beauty costume.

How was the costume different from other costumes you've designed?
Marvel Studios has the highest bar in the industry, so that's a challenge. It's a little bit daunting to any new designer that comes on board. On this particular costume, the challenge was the costume needed to be moveable, and she needed to be able perform during the action sequences.

The Kree have appeared previously in the Marvel Cinematic Universe. Are there differences in their costumes for this film, in particular Starforce?
The first thing was to make them look as believable as possible. We took the Kree colors – the teals, the greens – but in the other movies the Kree are not that prominent. [For this film, the Kree costumes] were designed based on the Captain Marvel costume, but different colors – black and teal. Each Starforce costume is different because they are a specialized force, like a Delta Force, and each has their own specialty, their own weapons. Each has a different star, different lines, different shoulders, and different weapons.

What was your approach to the Skrulls' costumes?
It's a very different issue than the Starforce oufits, because we have never met Skrulls in the other movies. In the comics, they are in purple jumpsuits and black underwear, so we didn't want that. The one thing that we kept from the Skrulls from the comics is the purple color.

The idea was to make them as different as possible from Starforce and, in a sense, all the other Marvel heroes. Through a lot of discussions and a lot of sketches and artwork, the decision was taken to make them be very asymmetrical, very organic, and not have all of the symmetry and straight and strong lines of other Marvel characters – because they do morph. But that presented a whole different challenge in making the costumes. When you have a symmetrical costume, you do one half and then you reverse it, as the human body is symmetrical. Here, we essentially had to do two costumes, because everything is different left to right – there are no defined lines.

Also, purple is a sensitive color, because it can go kind of unpleasant really quickly. We decided to go with a dark

> ## "The decision was taken to make the Skrulls be very asymmetrical, very organic."

09

purple, but there are a lot of scenes in the dark, so we made them shiny and interesting in texture and detail.

Were you surprised when you saw any of the costumes in action?
The first time we saw Starforce, it was like, "Oh, my God, this really works!" It was just amazing. When they are loading into the ship and they are all together, even for those of us that were deeply involved, it was: "Okay, it really works."

What kind of approach did you take in clothing the characters to fit in with the period settings of the film?
We have a little bit of '70s, a little more of '80s, and then the rest is the '90s, which sounds too recent to be period from the past! Working with the directors, Anna and Ryan, they were adamant that everything needed to look real. It was all about subtly giving nods to the period; we didn't go with the huge bell bottoms and the crazy hair for the '70s, or huge shoulders, because people in every one of those periods didn't wear stuff from the fashion magazines or crazy rock'n'roll stuff.

What are your most abiding memories of making *Captain Marvel*?
The whole movie was a big challenge for us in costumes. We had the '70s, '80s, and '90s. We had Captain Marvel, one Super Hero, but we really had six Super Heroes, the whole Starforce. Then we had a lot of Skrulls, and Talos as their leader and their technician. There was that whole world; then we had the world of Hala and the people of the Hala – two worlds, the subzone and the upper zone. We had the Supreme Intelligence. Then we had to go to a Torfan planet, so there were a Torfan people.

There were a lot of different worlds that we had to create, each of them completely different from the other, in color, in image, in texture, in everything. It was quite challenging for us, and at the same time a lot of fun. I hope that audiences enjoy it too.

What do you think audiences will take away from this film?
I'm sure they will have fun; I'm sure it's going to be very exciting. But I'm hoping that audiences are going to relate to Carol's story, her whole character arc. ○

06 The Skrulls hit the beach

07 The purple coloring of Talos and the Skrull costumes is a nod to the colors of the original comic books

08 Bron-Char in the teal, green armor of the Kree military

09 An armored squad of Skrulls

Kevin Feige

Marvel Studios President

The man who has overseen ten years of Marvel Studios movies discusses the introduction of Captain Marvel, a hero set to be at the forefront of the Marvel Cinematic Universe.

Captain Marvel: The Official Movie Special: Why did you feel the time was now right to bring Captain Marvel to the big screen?

Kevin Feige: In our comics mythology, Captain Marvel is a character who's got one foot on Earth and one foot in the cosmic arena. Now that we've made a number of movies that take place on Earth, and a number of cosmic adventures with the Avengers, the Guardians of the Galaxy, and Thor, we thought it was the right time to finally introduce Captain

Marvel to the world. She's one of the most powerful – and one of the most popular – characters in our comics, and will be the most powerful character in the Marvel Cinematic Universe.

Take us through Captain Marvel's powers and how they develop throughout the movie.

At the beginning of the film, Captain Marvel has a large amount of her power base. She's got super-strength; she's unbelievably fast; she's incredibly coordinated; she fights extremely well, and most importantly she has these photon blasts that come out of her hands. Over the course of the movie she'll get even more powerful, and eventually be able to fly. She'll be one of our primary characters who uses the power of flight.

Why did you choose Brie Larson for the role?

The great thing about Captain Marvel is she is a human. She's a real person, Carol Danvers, who gets these

> **"Captain Marvel is about to take the lead and be at the forefront of the entire Cinematic Universe."**

> ## "*Captain Marvel* has influenced everything that has happened in every movie you've seen already in the MCU."

01 Kevin Feige on set with *Ant-Man and the Wasp* director, Peyton Reed

02 A cat and mouse chase as Vers hunts a Skrull

03 Carol Danvers on the airfield

04 Brie Larson as Carol Danvers, a very human hero

incredible powers and who has these amazing adventures in outer space. But as with all of the best Marvel characters, she needs to be very human. So this is not just about somebody who is incredibly powerful and can fly around and shoot photon blasts out of her hands; it's somebody who's very human, who's very vulnerable, and who has multiple dimensions.

When we found out that Brie Larson might be interested in joining our world, we had a number of meetings. She was a huge fan of the character in the comics. One of the highlights of my career at Marvel was introducing her at Comic-Con and having her come out on stage and stand there with literally almost everybody else from our movies. There she was at the forefront, and it was a great foreshadowing – not just for how audiences are going to embrace Brie as this character, but also for how Captain Marvel is about to take the lead and be at the forefront of the entire Cinematic Universe.

What was it like, seeing Brie in her Captain Marvel costume for the first time?

In over 17 years at Marvel, I've had a number of amazing experiences seeing the actors wearing the costumes for the first time – you just get this sensation of, "I can't believe I'm looking at this in real life." When Robert Downey Jr. put on the Iron Man armor; when I saw the X-Men all together; when Chris Evans stepped into the Captain America suit; when Chris Hemsworth first held the hammer in full Thor regalia – even Chris Pratt putting on the Star-Lord outfit for the first time, and Scarlett Johansson in the Black Widow outfit: these were amazing, iconic moments.

We had the first full costume fitting with Brie Larson on the set of *Avengers: Endgame*, and just stepping into the little tent on set where we hide – because we don't want many people to see – it was astounding. Seeing that character that we've been working on for years, that we've been dreaming about even longer than that, seeing her standing in front of us for the first time, in real life – ▶

"This is an origin story about Carol Danvers and how she becomes Captain Marvel, but it's an origin story told in a very unique fashion."

▶ it's incredible. It's an amazing start for the adventure that lies ahead.

How important was it to have a female lead in a Marvel Studios movie?
We've always had powerful female characters and powerful female heroes in our movies, but having Captain Marvel as the title character for the first time feels like it's overdue. It's something that we are excited about and can't wait to deliver to the world.

What prompted you to set this movie in the 1990s?
Except for the origin of Captain America in the 1940s, *Captain Marvel* is set before the events of every other film in the Marvel Cinematic Universe. This film takes place in the 1990s for some very specific reasons – most of which are because we thought it would be a lot of fun to do a movie set in that period, to see what it's like for a woman who is a member of the Air Force, who has these dreams, who tries to compete in that world, and who does a pretty amazing job until certain things happen to her.

Also, to be able to see what the Marvel Cinematic Universe was like during that era before Iron Man became Iron Man, before anybody else came together as the Avengers, is very important to us. It is going to set the stage for how Captain Marvel has influenced everything that has happened in every movie you've seen already in the MCU.

One exciting aspect of *Captain Marvel* is the return of Nick Fury…
Carol Danvers – Captain Marvel – is the star of this movie. She's in almost every scene of this movie, some in outer space, some on Earth. There's a large cast of characters that we surround her with. One of those characters is Nick Fury.

Sam Jackson is coming back to play a younger version of Nick Fury. He's got both of his eyes – he hasn't lost that left eye yet, so he doesn't need the eye patch. He is a different Nick Fury. He's a Nick Fury who thinks his entire career as a spy within S.H.I.E.L.D. was about the Cold War and all of these earthbound situations that he had to deal with; and in the 1990s, the Berlin Wall has fallen. It seems as if the Cold War has ended, and perhaps his career is plateauing and there's not as much for him to do.

There's an event that occurs and signifies the arrival of Captain Marvel back on Earth, which thrusts him into a new adventure and leads him on the path to become the Nick Fury we know and have seen in all the other movies. But at this point he's never seen an alien. He doesn't think any of that stuff is real. We get to see his first encounter with cosmic events – with supernatural, superhuman events.

07

How do you balance the different milieus of the movie?

This is an origin story about Carol Danvers and how she becomes Captain Marvel, but it's an origin story told in a very unique fashion. We meet her for the first time as Captain Marvel with her power base in outer space, as part of a team called Starforce, working for the Kree Empire. Throughout the course of the first act, some events occur with the Skrulls – the new enemy that we're introducing into the Marvel Cinematic Universe for the very first time – and she finds herself on Earth. She thinks it's an alien planet to her, but slowly, surely, memories start coming back. We realize she's human. She's from Earth. Her origins happened here on Earth in the 1990s.

We get to have a lot of fun with the time period. She crashes right into a Blockbuster Video store at the start of the movie. There's some fun to be had with that time period, with Carol beginning as a fish out of water, until we begin to peel back the layers. She realizes she's human, this was her origin, and we begin to uncover the mystery of what happened to her.

What made the Skrulls the right choice to be the villains in this film?

We've talked about the Skrulls since the very earliest days at Marvel Studios, figuring out when and where to introduce them. They might be the most famous alien race in Marvel Comics. They're shape-shifters; they're green; they've got pointy ears. They are very important to the mythology of our comics universe, going back decades.

This Captain Marvel story was the right one to bring them into the fold and to introduce the overarching narrative of the Kree-Skrull War, which is one of the most important and groundbreaking storylines in the Marvel comics. That will be the backdrop to the adventures of Captain Marvel.

What made you choose Anna Boden and Ryan Fleck as directors?

We love to look outside the box for filmmakers, although for us it's not really outside the box: it's just finding talented people who might not have done movies on this scale or size before, but who've done incredibly clever, unique, special films. Anna Boden and Ryan Fleck have done just that. They've done a number of films that impressed us and show a very firm guiding hand and vision of storytelling.

We met with them three or four times, and they just understood Carol. They understood her story and the wish-fulfillment of that journey of becoming a hero. The work they've done on this character – being a big part of hiring Brie, working with Brie now – is very special. We have very high hopes. ○

> **"This Captain Marvel story was the right one to bring the Skrulls into the fold and to introduce the overarching narrative of the Kree-Skrull War."**

05 Captain Marvel, a hero who is "long overdue" according to Kevin Feige

06 The Kree under fire

07 Carol Danvers' story is a journey of wish fulfillment according to Feige

"I keep saying to myself, 'I can't believe this is me. I can't believe I lucked out this way.' I remember every cameo I've done since the first movie. I think I'm a very lucky guy."

Stan Lee 1922 - 2018

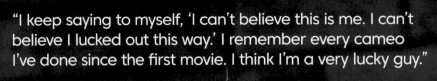